SQL Design Patterns
The Expert Guide to SQL Programming

IT In-Focus Series

Vadim Tropashko

"Complexity is easy; simplicity is hard."

Edmund Kean

SQL Design Patterns
The Expert Guide to SQL Programming

By Vadim Tropashko

Copyright © 2006 by Rampant TechPress. All rights reserved.

Printed in the United States of America.

Published in Kittrell, North Carolina, USA.

IT In-Focus Series: Book #4

Series Editor: Donald K. Burleson

Editors: Janet Burleson, John Lavender, and Robin Haden

Cover Design: Janet Burleson

Printing History: October 2006 for First Edition

Many of the designations used by computer vendors to distinguish their products are claimed as Trademarks. All names known by Rampant TechPress to be trademark names appear in this text as initial caps.

ISBN: 0-9776715-4-2

Library of Congress Control Number: 2006934082

Table of Contents

Conventions Used in this Book

It is critical for any technical publication to follow rigorous standards and employ consistent punctuation conventions to make the text easy to read.

However, this is not an easy task. Within SQL there are many types of notation that can confuse a reader. It is also important to remember that many SQL commands are case sensitive, and are always left in their original executable form, and never altered with italics or capitalization.

Parameters - All SQL command arguments and parameters will be *italics*.

Variables – All program variables and arguments will also remain in *italics*.

Programs & Products – All products and programs that are known to the author are capitalized according to the vendor specifications (IBM, Microsoft, etc). All names known by Rampant TechPress to be trademark names appear in this text as initial caps. References to Oracle and SQL Server are in Title case.

Acknowledgements

I want to thank Gabe Romanescu, Bob Badour, Don Burleson, Vladimir Barriere, Anton Tropashko, and Gary Howard as they were so generous with their time to comment on early drafts of this work. Marshall Spight and John Garmany went above and beyond the call of duty in providing a detailed review of the entire manuscript.

Many other people's SQL solutions are credited throughout this book. Finally, I thank many Usenet forums posters (who unfortunately remain unaccredited) for being a source of challenging SQL problems. Thanks to all the people at Rampant who were involved in the process of completing this book. It could never have happened this way without you.

I also want to thank and acknowledge everyone who helped bring this book to fruition:

Janet Burleson, for her production management, including the coordination of the cover art, page proofing, printing, and distribution.

Teri Wade, for her help in the production of the page proofs.

John Lavender, for his assistance with the web site, and for creating the code depot and the online shopping cart for this book.

Jennifer Adkins, for her help with sales and distribution.

Many thanks,

Vadim

Preface

SQL is a very successful language. Yet, is there a place for an advanced SQL book in the era of "Learn Technology X in 10 Minutes"? Indeed, the tech industry today emphasizes a shallow knowledge of a huge number of technical skills, rather than deep knowledge of a more specialized skill. That's how workers have been getting jobs, by knowing a tiny bit of many skills employers might need. Someone who knows how to use SQL in an advanced way does not have a proportionate advantage in getting a job over someone who knows only the basics. If this second person, however, also knows J2EE, XSLT, Ajax, Flash, or any other flash in the pan to a similarly basic level, then he or she has a greater employment advantage.

The major flaw of this line of reason is equating the sophistication of SQL to these rather unsound technologies. This might be surprising to a newcomer who generally finds SQL a little bit old fashioned compared to the "modern" programming languages. It is almost as old as C, which spawned at least 3 newer generation languages already, and it looks like COBOL, so why isn't it obsolete yet? Let me assure you that this appearance is misleading. Under the cover of sloppy and archaic syntax, a high abstraction language is found.

SQL programming is very unusual from the procedural perspective: there is no explicit flow control, no loops and no variables either to apply operations to or to store intermediate results into. SQL heavily leverages predicates instead, which elevates it to Logic Programming. Then, the grouping and aggregation syntax blends naturally into this already formidable logic foundation. Anybody who rediscovers that matrix or polynomial multiplication can be written in just three lines of code has a long lasting impression.

These ingredients that make SQL unique partially explain why advanced SQL programming does not revolve around syntax features, but demands a SQL programmer to develop an ability to recognize complex patterns. Yes, beyond a certain point a skill of piling up subqueries does not give much of a return and one has to study some rudimentary theory, which classifies known SQL solutions into patterns.

Patterns in procedural[1] programming became popular a decade ago, originated with a landmark book by Gamma et. al.[2] Each pattern has its name so that developers could quickly refer to it by just a name. "Oh, that's a singleton!" instead of a lengthy description and often accompanied with a code snippet.

Patterns received a sour reception in a high abstraction language community. The prevailing perception was that patterns are a signature of low level programming. When a programmer sees patterns in her programs, it is a sign of trouble. The shape of a program should reflect only the problem it needs to solve. Any other regularity in the code indicates that abstractions are not powerful enough.

In reality, however, any language is quite limited in its abstraction power, declarative languages notwithstanding. Sooner or later we have to find workarounds for those limitations. This is how SQL patterns were born!

Patterns greatly improve our communication capabilities. On internet SQL forums it is not uncommon for people to ask the same question over and over again. Pattern names such as *Interval coalesce* or *Relational division*, for example, rarely surface in the discussion thread, giving way to numerous reply messages pointlessly competing to see who can find a query that does not look intimidating. Patterns allow succinct replies like this: "Lookup the *Interval coalesce* method in the … textbook".

---

[1] *Procedural* or low abstraction (e.g. C++ or Java) as opposed to *declarative* or high-abstraction (e.g. SQL). Object-oriented features don't qualify a language above the procedural status.

[2] The "Gang of Four" book: Erich Gamma, Richard Helm, Ralph Johnson, John Vlissides. Design Patterns. Addison-Wesley, 1995

Establishing common pattern names is the first goal of this book. Most of the patterns have standard names: *Skyline query*, *Pivot*, or *Nested Intervals*, for example. Few do not; we have to work out a name, like the fancy sounding *Discrete interval sampling*, for example.

When presenting SQL patterns in this book I decided to dismiss the standard template form. Template is perfect for reference material, but is a nuisance for a textbook. More important than this stylistic comment, however, is the fact that fairly soon you might stumble into patterns that require little familiarity with undergraduate level math. Don't be discouraged, however: as John Garmany suggested, many topics start making sense on second reading. In the *Indicator Functions* section, for example, you may want to skip the theory, first, rewind to the sample problem and SQL solutions, then, rollback to the theory.

List of patterns

- Counting
- Conditional summation
- Integer generator
- String/Collection decomposition
- List Aggregate
- Enumerating pairs
- Enumerating sets
- Interval coalesce
- Discrete interval sampling
- User-defined aggregate
- Pivot
- Symmetric difference
- Histogram

- Skyline query
- Relational division
- Outer union
- Complex constraint
- Nested intervals
- Transitive closure
- Hierarchical total

Counting in SQL

Introduction

Counting is one of the basic patterns that a SQL developer learns after learning the basics: selection, projection, join, and subquery. While counting might look deceptively easy in a context of a single table, it becomes intellectually challenging when two tables are joined together and grouping is applied.

The first half of this chapter will present information to enable the reader to write counting queries in a complex context.

The second half of the chapter will present information regarding *conditional summation*. This pattern is a beautiful combination of two SQL constructs: the *case* operator, and *aggregation*. Conditional summation has numerous applications, which will also be presented throughout the remainder of the chapter.

Counting Ordered Rows

Let's start with a basic counting problem. Suppose we are given a list of integers, for example:

x
2
3
4
6
9

and want to enumerate all of them sequentially like this:

x	#
2	1
3	2
4	3
6	4
9	5

Enumerating rows in the increasing order is the same as counting the number of rows preceding a given row.

SQL enjoys success unparalleled by any rival query language. The reason for such popularity might be credited to its proximity to the English[3] language. Examine the informal idea carefully:

Enumerating rows in increasing order is counting how many rows precede a given row.

Perhaps the most important thing to note is the rows in the source table are referred to twice: first, to a *given* row, and second, to a *preceding* row. Therefore, the number list must be joined with itself as shown in Figure 1.1.

---

[3] This proximity partially explains why newer relational languages had such a limited success. For example, Tutorial D has a succinct notation, better NULL handling, and pure set semantics. These are not breakthrough features however; a New and Improved query language had better be leaps and bounds ahead, not just simpler to type.

Surprisingly, not many basic SQL tutorials, which are so abundant on the web today, mention a Cartesian product. A Cartesian product is a *join* operator with no join condition[4]

select A.*, B.* from A, B

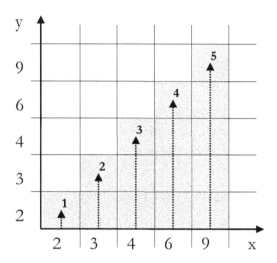

Figure 1.1 - *Cartesian product of the set $A = \{2,3,4,6,9\}$ by itself. Counting all the elements x that are no greater than y produces the sequence number of y in the set A.*

Carrying over this idea into a formal SQL query is straightforward. As it is the first query in this book, it will be performed step by step. The Cartesian product itself is:

```
select t.x x, tt.x y⁵
from T t, T tt
```

---

[4] Many DBAs would jump in pointing that queries with a Cartesian product are inefficient, but the rule of thumb of avoiding a Cartesian product is just too simplistic.

[5] We use Oracle syntax and write <column expr> <alias> instead of ANSI SQL <column expr> AS <alias>. Ditto for table expressions.

The triangle area below the main diagonal is:

```
select t.x x, tt.x y
from T t, T tt
where tt.x <= t.x
```

And finally, only one column is needed – *t.x* – to group the previous result by and count:

```
select t.x, count(*) seqNum
from T t, T tt
where tt.x <= t.x
group by t.x
```

There is a certain harmony of *group by* operator in a joint effort with relational *join*. There are also drawbacks that we'll discuss later.

Equivalence Relation and Group By

Almost any other SQL query uses the *group by* operator. Why is the *group by* operator so powerful? It is not among the fundamental relational algebra operators. A partial answer to this fascinating efficiency is that *group by* embodies an equivalence relation. Indeed, it partitions rows into equivalence classes of rows with identical values in a column or a group of columns, and calculates aggregate values per each equivalence class.

So what happens if the programmer modifies the problem slightly and asks for a list of pairs where each number is coupled with its predecessor?

x	predecessor
2	
3	2
4	3
6	4
9	6

Let me provide a typical mathematician's answer, which is remarkable in a certain way. Given that it has already been shown how to number list elements successively, it might be tempting to reduce the current problem to the previous one:

Enumerate all the numbers in the increasing order and match each sequence number seq# with predecessor seq#-1. Next!

This attitude is, undoubtedly, the most economical way of thinking, although not necessarily producing the most efficient SQL. Therefore, let's revisit our original approach, as illustrated on Figure 1.2.

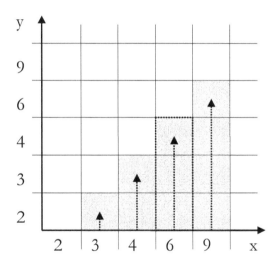

Figure 1.2 - *Cartesian product of the set $A = \{2,3,4,6,9\}$ by itself. The predecessor of y is the maximal number in a set of x that are less than y. There is no predecessor for y = 2.*

This translates into the following SQL query:

```
select t.x, max(tt.x) predecessor
from T t, T tt
where tt.x < t.x
group by t.x
```

Both solutions are expressed in a standard SQL leveraging join and grouping with aggregation. Alternatively, instead of joining and grouping why not simply calculate the *count* or *max* in place as a *correlated scalar* subquery:

```
select t.x,
       (select count(*) from T tt where tt.x <= t.x) seq#
from T t
group by t.x
```

The subquery always returns a single value; this is why it is called scalar. The *tt.x <= t.x* predicate connects it to the outer query; this is why it is called correlated. Arguably, leveraging correlated scalar subqueries is one the most intuitive techniques in writing SQL queries.

Is GROUP BY Redundant?

Chris Date[6] asserts that the *group by* operator is redundant since

select deptno, avg(sal) from Emp

group by deptno

could be rewritten as:

select distinct deptno,

    (select avg(sal) from Emp ee

      where e.deptno = ee.deptno)

from Emp e

---

[6] C. J. Date, *Relational Database Writings*, 1994-1997, Addison Wesley.

> Unlike Date, who exploits this fact as evidence of SQL deficiencies, it is rather viewed as yet another demonstration of the power of scalar subqueries.

How about counting rows that are not necessarily distinct? This is where the method breaks. It is challenging to distinguish duplicate rows by purely logical means, so various less "pure" counting methods were devised. They all, however, require extending the SQL syntactically, which was the beginning of slipping along the ever increasing language complexity slope.

Here is how an analytic SQL extension counts rows:

```
select x, rank() over(order by x) seq# from T; -- first problem
select x, lag() over(order by x) seq# from T; -- second problem
```

Many people suggest that not only is it more efficient, but more intuitive. The idea that "analytics rock" can be challenged in many ways. The syntactic clarity has its cost: the SQL programmer has to remember (or, at least, lookup) the list of analytic functions. The performance argument is not evident, since non-analytical queries are a simpler construction from the optimizer perspective. A shorter list of physical execution operators implies fewer query transformation rules, and less dramatic combinatorial explosion of the optimizer search space.

It might even be argued that the syntax could be better. The *partition by* and *order by* clauses have similar functionality to the *group by* and *order by* clauses in the main query block. Yet one name was reused, and the other had been chosen to receive a new name. Unlike other *scalar* expressions, which can be placed anywhere in SQL query where scalar values are accepted, the analytics clause lives in the scope of the *select* clause only. I have never been able to suppress an impression that analytic extension could be designed in more natural way.

Conditional Summation with CASE Operator

The genesis of the conditional summation idiom is an equivalence between *count(*)* and *sum(1)*. Formally,

```
select count(*) from emp
```

is the same as:

```
select sum(1) from emp
```

There is must be something wrong here. How these two queries can be equivalent? They produce different result when the *Emp* relation is empty.

This is merely a misfortunate historical artifact. Had SQL ANSI standard committee been in a mathematical mood that day, they would certainly fixed the definition to make them equivalent. This would make SQL world a tiny bit simpler.

More important, however, is a common misconception that *count* should have any arguments at all. First, for most practical purposes *count = sum(1)*, and there is no free variable parameter within the *sum(1)* expression. Second, think about how the *count* function may be implemented on a low-level. A reasonable code must look like this:

```
int count = 0;
for( int i = 0; i< 10; i++)
    count = count + 1;
```

The count variable is updated during each row processing with the unary increment operator *+1*. Unlike *count*, any "normal" aggregation has to use a binary operation during each aggregate incremental computation step

```
int sum = 0;
for( int i = 0; i< 10; i++)
    sum = sum + element[i];
```

that is, + for *sum*, $\vee$ for *max*, $\wedge$ for *min*, etc. Therefore, one argument is needed for normal aggregates, and no arguments for *count*.

Argument for COUNT

The formal difference between

select count(*) from emp

and

select count(1) from emp

has been the subject of lengthy investigations on some internet forums. If there were indeed any implementation and performance difference between the two, then one can argue that the query optimizer should transform the query accordingly to eliminate it. In other words, this counting syntax quirk is not worth 2 cents[7].

OK, as far as simple counting is concerned, there does not appear to be any need for an argument. But what about

```
select count(ename) from emp
```

where only *non-null* values of the *ename* column are counted? The description of *count(ename)* in the previous sentence translates directly into SQL:

```
select count(*) from emp where ename is not null
```

---

[7] In oracle you can witness that such transformation indeed has taken place by examining the `plan_table.projection` column:

```
explain plan for select count(1) from dual;

PROJECTION
---------
(#keys=0) COUNT(*)[22]
```

So, *count(ename)* is no more than a syntax shortcut.

Well, how about

```
select count(distinct ename) from emp
```

where the *count* aggregate function accepts a column expression with a keyword? This is yet another shortcut:

```
select count(*) from (
    select distinct empno from emp
)
```

What if counting two different values at the same time like this is preferred:

```
select count(ename), count(*) from emp
```

Even though it looks like SQL has a dedicated syntax shortcut for every imaginable task, at this point it is easy to argue that these extensions are nifty at least in some practical cases.

Enter the *conditional summation* pattern. Whenever rows are counted satisfying a certain criteria such as

```
select count(*) from emp
where sal < 1000
```

and the *where* clause seems to hinder the query's evolution to a more sophisticated form, it can be rewritten without the *where* clause:

```
select sum(case when sal < 1000 then 1 else 0 end)
from emp
```

Conditional summation queries scale up nicely to accommodate more complex requirements. In the example with the familiar *Emp* table,

DEPTNO	ENAME	SAL
10	MILLER	1300
10	CLARK	2450
10	KING	5000
20	SMITH	800
20	ADAMS	1100
20	JONES	2975
20	SCOTT	3000
20	FORD	3000
30	JAMES	950
30	MARTIN	1250
30	WARD	1250
30	TURNER	1500
30	ALLEN	1600
30	BLAKE	2850

the previous query is transformed to count the small salaries per each department by amending it with *group by*:

```
select deptno,
       sum(case when sal < 1000 then 1 else 0 end) cnt
from emp
group by deptno
```

DEPTNO	CNT
30	1
20	1
10	0

The subtle novelty here is that the conditional summation query is no longer equivalent to the former attempt restricting the condition in the *where* clause:

```
select deptno,count(*) from emp
where sal < 1000
group by deptno
```

DEPTNO	COUNT(*)
30	1
20	1

Zero counts were perfectly legal in the aggregation without the grouping case. Disappearing zeros are a sign of (yet another) SQL inconsistency.

Aggregation without Grouping

An aggregation with no grouping is, in fact, an aggregation within a single group. If SQL syntax allowed grouping by the empty set of columns $\varnothing$ [8], then a simple aggregate

select count(*) from T

could also be represented as

select count(*) from T

group by $\varnothing$

Without the empty set syntax, we still can write

select count(*) from T

group by 0

The *0* pseudo column is a constant expression, so that the table T is partitioned into a single group effectively the same way as with the empty set.

Perhaps the most important rationalization for the conditional summation idiom is counting by different criteria. Without conditional summation we would have to count by each individual condition in a

---

[8] Or, rather, a less "ASCII-challenged" notation {}

dedicated query block, and combine those counts with a join. The *pivot* operator, which will be studied in Chapter 3, is a typical showcase of this idea.

Before the *case* operator became widely available in off-the-shelf RDBMS systems, a much more ingenious counting method with an indicator function was employed.

Indicator and Step Functions

An indicator function[9] $1_A(x)$ maps every element x of a set A into 1, and any element which is not in A into 0. Formally:

$$1_A(x) := \text{if } x \in A \text{ then } 1 \text{ else } 0 \text{ endif}$$

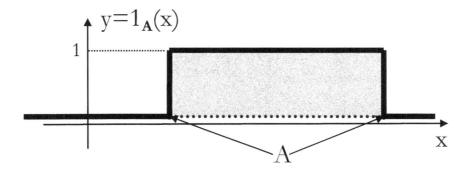

Figure 1.3 - *Indicator function $1_A(x)$.*

Set operations can be expressed in terms of indicator functions. Intersection is as simple as multiplication:

---

[9] The indicator function is sometimes also called characteristic function, although this usage is much less frequent now.

$$1_{A\cap B}(x) = 1_A(x)\,1_B(x)$$

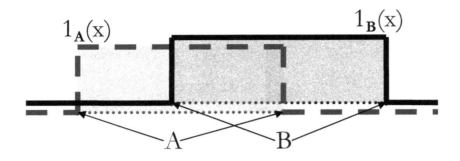

Figure 1.4 - *Indicator functions $1_A(x)$ and $1_B(x)$.*

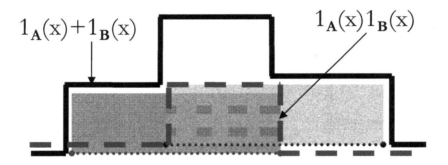

Figure 1.5 - *$1_A(x)1_B(x)$ is an indicator function for $A\cap B$. However, $1_A(x)+1_B(x)$ is not an indicator function, because it is equal to 2 for any $x \in A\cap B$. By inclusion-exclusion principle we have to subtract $1_A(x)1_B(x)$.*

Unlike set theory where union is dual to intersection, there is no duality between multiplication and addition of indicator functions. Therefore, union has to be expressed via the *inclusion-exclusion principle* as:

$$1_{A \cup B}(x) = 1_A(x) + 1_B(x) - 1_A(x)\, 1_B(x)$$

In SQL context, the indicator function's domain is a set of numbers. An indicator function for a set $x \in [0,\infty)$ is a very important special case. It is called (a primitive) *step* function, and has a designated notation:

$$1_x := 1_{[0,\infty)}(x)$$

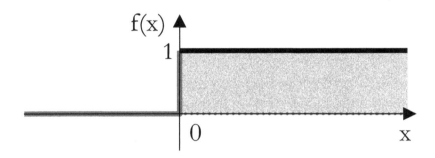

1.6 - *Step function f(x)=1ₓ.*

Let's also write the primitive step function definition in pseudo programming notation, which was used for the indicator function in the very beginning of the session

$$1_x := \text{if } x \geq 0 \text{ then } 1 \text{ else } 0 \text{ endif}$$

If the abstraction level is raised and the hard coded constants 0, 1 and yet another 0, is converted into variables,

$$\text{if } x \geq x_0 \text{ then } \alpha \text{ else } \beta \text{ endif}$$

then the pseudo code starts looking similar to the *case* operator. This expression is a generic step function (although it doesn't have any abbreviated notation).

The generic step function can be expressed via the primitive step function:

$$\text{if } x \geq x_0 \text{ then } \alpha \text{ else } \beta \text{ endif} = \alpha\, 1_{x-x_0} + \beta\, 1_{x_0-x}$$

So far, so good handling simple case operators, but what about nested *case* expressions? Consider the following:

$$\text{if } x \geq 0 \text{ then (if } y \geq 0 \text{ then 1 else 0 endif) else 0 endif}$$

Easy: the above formula for general step function should handle the case where α is an expression rather than a constant. By substitution we have

$$\text{if } x \geq 0 \text{ then (if } y \geq 0 \text{ then 1 else 0 endif) else 0 endif} = 1_y\, 1_x$$

as if we had just an intersection of the $x \geq 0$ and $y \geq 0$ sets!

However, still missing is a way to express the step function in SQL. True, we can trivially utilize the *case* operator, but then we can hardly justify learning the step and indicator functions. The key formula is expressing the step function via the standard numeric *sign* function:

```
step(x) := sign(1+sign(x))
```

Now queries with conditional expressions can be written in a peculiar way:

```
select ename, sal,
       sign(1+sign(sal-2000)) SALgt2000 -- i.e. step(x-2000)
from emp
```

ENAME	SAL	SALgt2000
SMITH	800	0

ALLEN	1600	0
WARD	1250	0
JONES	2975	1
MARTIN	1250	0
BLAKE	2850	1
CLARK	2450	1
SCOTT	3000	1
KING	5000	1
TURNER	1500	0
ADAMS	1100	0
JAMES	950	0
FORD	3000	1
MILLER	1300	0

The step function method was the only game in town a long time ago when the *case* operator was not part of the SQL standard yet[10]. Nowadays a seasoned SQL programmer writes a *case* expression without giving it a second thought. Yet, there are rare cases when clever application of indicator function is still a contender. Consider the following data:

```
select * from Transactions
```

Date	Amount	Type
01-01-2005	800	debit
01-01-2005	1600	credit
01-01-2005	1400	credit
01-01-2005	200	debit
01-02-2005	250	debit
01-02-2005	150	debit
01-02-2005	850	credit

You are asked to sum transaction quantities grouped by *Date* to produce the output like this:

---

[10] SQL technique of indicator and step functions is credited to David Rozenshtein, Anatoly Abramovich, and Eugene Birger

Date	debit	credit
01-01-2005	1000	3000
01-02-2005	400	850

The first step towards a solution is recognizing the indicator function hidden in the above data. The character *Type* column is very inconvenient to deal with; can it be transformed into numeric? The two value column certainly can be coded with numbers, but that is not what we are looking for. It is the *instr(Type, 'debit')* and *instr(Type, 'credit')* expressions that convert the character column values into indicator functions. We proceed by simply summarizing the *Amount* weighted by indicator functions:

```
select Date,
       sum(Amount*instr(Type,'debit')) debit,
       sum(Amount*instr(Type,'credit')) credit
from Transactions
group by Date
```

This nice solution is due to Laurent Schneider. Compare it to a conditional summation with the *case* operator[11]:

```
select Date,
       sum(case when Type='debit' then Amount else 0 end) debit,
       sum(case when Type='credit' then Amount else 0 end) credit
from Transactions
group by Date
```

A Case for the CASE Operator

This section embarks upon a little bit longer journey. We have already mentioned SQL proximity to the English language. Consider the following query:

---

[11] In chapter 3 we'll learn the conventional name for this problem: the *pivot* pattern.

For each customer, show the number of calls made during the first 6 months that exceeded the average length of all calls made during the year, and the number of calls made during the second 6 months that exceeded the same average length.[12]

True, you have to read this long sentence more than once. Upon careful examination, though, you'll be easily convinced that the apparent complexity is illusory. The query can be translated into SQL in small increments. But first, a schema is needed to anchor the SQL query to:

```
table Calls (
    FromPh      integer(10),
    ToPh        integer(10),
    ConnectedAt date,
    Length      integer
);
```

The *Calls* table stores the calls placed on a telephone network over a period of one year. Each *FromPh* number identifies a customer.

Thus the process begins with translating

For each customer ...

Into

```
select FromPh, …
from Calls
group by FromPh
```

The missing part that will be gradually developed in the next steps is intentionally marked with ellipsis.

At this moment you may wonder if

```
select distinct FromPh
from Calls
```

---

[12] Adopted from paper by Damianos Chantziantoniou and Kenneth Ross: Querying Multiple Features of Groups in Relational Databases. http://www.dmst.aueb.gr/damianos/vldb96-acc.ps

is the easier way to list all the customers. It certainly is, but now what? This query is complete, it answers the question partially, but it cannot be expanded to answer the remainder. The *group by* clause, on the other hand, is one of the most powerful SQL constructs.

DISTINCT operator is redundant

Technically, the *distinct* operator is a special case of *group by*. For any table (or view) T

select distinct x, y from T

is equivalent to

select x, y from T

group by x, y

The next clause

..., show the number of calls made during the first 6 months that exceeded the average length of all calls made during the year, ...

leaves us a choice. The condition can be placed into the *where* clause, but then some difficulty may arise in assembling the query pieces together. A better alternative is to leverage a familiar conditional summation pattern:

```
select FromPh,
       sum( case when … then 1 else 0 end ),
       …
from Calls
group by FromPh
```

Ellipsis means that the condition must be interpreted:

... during the first 6 months that exceeded the average length of all calls made during the year ...

This is still a relatively complex sentence. You may notice that the two variables: *ConnectedAt* and *Length* are involved. The condition begins with

… during the first 6 months …

which is easily translated into *ConnectedAt* < *'1-July-2005'*. The next fragment

… the average length of all calls made during the year …

is a little bit trickier. First, the query is ambiguous. Did the author mean the average length of all the calls in the system, or the average length for each customer? Both interpretations are perfectly reasonable. The average length of the call is

```
select avg(Length)
from Calls
```

while the average length of the call per each customer is

```
select FromPh,
       avg(Length)
from Calls
group by FromPh
```

The first interpretation is easier to implement than the second one, therefore, it is used as an exercise for the reader.

So, given the query that has been developed so far

```
select FromPh,
       sum( case when … then 1 else 0 end ),
       …
from Calls
group by FromPh
```

where does the relation

```
select FromPh,
       avg(Length)
from Calls
group by FromPh
```

fit in? The only place that admits arbitrary relations is the *from* clause.

Relational Closure

The SQL query block inside the *from* clause is called *inner view*. From a logical perspective there is no difference if a relation within the *from* clause (or anywhere in the SQL statement, for that matter) is a table or a view. It is a manifestation of the fundamental property of the Relational Model – Relational Closure. It is common to organize a query in a chain of inner views so that every step is small and easily comprehendible.

Let's nest the second query into the first as an inner view:

```
select c1.FromPh,
       sum( case when … then 1 else 0 end ),
       …
from Calls /*as*/ c1, (
    select FromPh,
           avg(Length) /*as*/ av
    from Calls
    group by FromPh
) c2
group by FromPh
```

Aliases *c1*, *c2*, and *av*, were introduced along the way, which will be helpful for further development. The *c1*, in fact, is required to disambiguate the *FromPh* column name in the *select* clause.

Translation of the informal query into SQL is only a few steps away from completion. First, the relations *c1* and *c2* are naturally joined by the customer id, *FromPh*. Second, the *av* alias is the average length of the call per each customer that was required to complete the predicate inside the *case* operator. Thus:

```
select c1.FromPh,
       sum(case when ConnectedAt < '1-July-2005'
                 and Length < av
             then 1 else 0 end),
       …
from Calls /*as*/ c1, (
    select FromPh,
           avg(Length) /*as*/ av
    from Calls
    group by FromPh
) c2
where c1.FromPh = c2.FromPh
group by FromPh
```

The final clause of the informal query

…and the number of calls made during the second 6 months that exceeded the same average length.

is very similar to the clause that was just analyzed.

Let's explore a slightly different path. Instead of introducing an inner view *c2*, why not calculate the average length for the customer in place as a correlated scalar subquery:

```
select c1.FromPh,
       sum(case when ConnectedAt < '1-July-2005'
            and Length < (
                          select avg(Length)
                          from Calls c2
                          where c1.FromPh = c2.FromPh
                )
            then 1 else 0 end
       ),
       …
from Calls c1
group by FromPh
```

Which of the two queries, the one with inner view, or the one with scalar subquery performs better? Well, they are logically equivalent, aren't they? The SQL engine reserves the right to transform a query to a logically equivalent one. A curious reader might want to check if both queries have the same execution plans on the RDBMS of his choice.

Let's pause and reflect back a little. The genesis of the solution is the *case* operator inside the *sum* aggregate. It is possible to express this query in SQL without it. Chantziantoniou et al (the authors of the article where I borrowed the problem from) followed that route and introduced a chain of named intermediate views[13] as follows:

```
create view AvgCallLengthPerCust as
select FromPh, avg(Length) /*as*/ avgL
from Calls
group by FromPh

create view ExcAvgDuring1stHalfYear as
select C.FromPh, count(*) /*as*/ count
from Calls /*as*/ C, AvgCallLengthPerCust /*as*/ V
where C.FromPh = V.FromPh AND
Length > avgL AND Date<'1-July-2005'
group by C.FromPh

create view ExcAvgDuring2ndHalfYear as
select C.FromPh, count(*) /*as*/ count
from Calls /*as*/ C, AvgCallLengthPerCust /*as*/ V
where C.FromPh = V.FromPh AND
Length > avgL AND Date>='1-July-2005'
group by C.FromPh

select a1.FromPh, a1.cnt, a2.cnt
from ExcAvgDuring1stHalfYear /*as*/ a1,
     ExcAvgDuring2ndHalfYear /*as*/ a2
where a1.FromPh=a2.FromPh
```

Based on this example, Chantziantoniou et al proposed extending SQL language in such a way that would make writing queries involving multiple features of the same group easier. As have been shown earlier, a solution leveraging the *case* operator makes this argument less convincing.

Summarizing by more than one Relation

The previous section mentioned that

```
select deptno, count(*) from Emp
group by deptno
```

---

[13] Instead of piling inner views inside of single, but big and messy SQL query

could be rewritten into an equivalent form leveraging the correlated scalar subquery:

```
select distinct deptno,
       (select count(*) from Emp ee
        where ee.deptno = e.deptno)
from Emp e
```

Both queries project the *Emp* relation onto the *deptno* column, and extend the result with one extra column that counts the number of rows in each group in the original relation. What about those *deptno* values that are missing in the *Emp* table, shouldn't they be listed with count 0? Suppose *deptno*, say, 40 is a valid department on the system, how can the query be changed to show it with the count 0?

Well, if *deptno = 40* is a valid department, then it should be in some table -- *Dept*, for example, where it is most likely a primary key. Then, why not use this table in the outer query:

```
select deptno,
       (select count(*) from Emp e
        where e.deptno = d.deptno)
from Dept d
```

An added bonus of having two tables in the query is that the *distinct* qualifier is no longer required.

Hugh Darwen's Summarize

Hugh Darwen argued[14] that *group by* with aggregation is an operator that requires two tables as the arguments, in general. The idea of introducing such an operator in SQL never caught on. Yet, in each practical situation it might be useful to double check if writing the *group by* clause as a one- or two- argument operator is more appropriate.

---

[14] C. J. Date, Relational Database Writings, 1994-1997, Addison Wesley.

SQL is notorious for allowing multiple ways to express the same query. Listing all the departments with the employee counts could also be rewritten via the outer join:

```
select d.deptno, d.dname,
       sum(case when e.deptno is not null then 1 else 0 end)
from Emp e right outer join Dept d
where d.deptno = e.deptno
group by d.deptno, d.dname
```

If the conditional summation pattern is reduced to a simple *count(*)*, then the departments with no employees will count 1 employee instead of 0.

ANSI Join Syntax

It is difficult to argue about elegance or ugliness of a certain syntax construction. You just see it or you don't. Comma separated join syntax reflects the fundamental feature of Relational Algebra, which asserts the normal form for select-project-join queries. The only kind of join that escapes it (and therefore, warrants a dedicated syntax) is the outer join.

It is not only aesthetics. It is common for production databases to have columns like CREATED_ON, or COMMENTS across many tables. In this case the NATURAL JOIN syntax is plain dangerous.

As Anthony Molinaro eloquently put it: "Old style is short and sweet and perfect. ANSI dumbed it down, and for people who've been developing for sometime, it's wholly unnecessary."

Which form, scalar subquery or outer join, is more performant? Surely, the answer differs between the vendors. Oracle, for example, is better at outer join optimization than unnesting scalar subqueries in the *select* clause[15]. Outer join from the optimizer's perspective has almost the same rights as normal join. It can be permuted with the other joins in the join order; it is costed similarly, etc. If the summarizing query is a

---

[15] This may certainly change as soon as Oracle implements scalar subquery unnesting.

part of the other query, chances are the optimizer may find the better plan when the query is written via outer join.

Interval Coalesce

Normally, the shorter the problem statement is, the simpler its formal expression in SQL. However, there are notable exceptions and *interval coalesce*[16] is one of them.

Given a set of intervals, return the smallest set of intervals that cover them.

This deceptively simple formulation leaves a pile of questions. First, what is the intervals table? This one is easy:

```
table Intervals (
   x integer, -- start of the interval
   y integer  -- end   of the interval
);

ALTER TABLE Intervals
ADD CONSTRAINT ends_ordering CHECK( x < y );
```

Perhaps, the *from* and *to*, or maybe, *start* and *end* column names may sound more appropriate. Unfortunately, they are SQL keywords.

Next, what is the concept of one interval covering the other? Easy: an interval is a set of points between the interval endpoints x and y. What about the endpoints, are they included into the interval? For our purpose, let's agree that both x and y belong to interval set of points, in other words, the intervals are closed from both ends. Open and half-open intervals require careful reexamination of all the inequality predicates in the query which we are going to write. Therefore, formally: $A = \{p \,|\, x \leq p \leq y\}$. Finally, interval A covers interval B when B is subset of A: $B \subseteq A$.

---

[16] There are two terms in the literature. "Developing Time-Oriented Database Applications in SQL" by R. Snodgrass uses *interval coalesce*, while "Temporal Data and The Relational Model" by C. Date et al calls it *interval packing*.

Armed with these definitions, we are ready to write the query. The *Intervals* table is the only candidate to be placed into the query *from* clause, but there is a catch. If we just select some intervals out of the set we have, we won't get the answer. Think about an easy case of two overlapping intervals. The answer to the query is an interval whose endpoints are combined from different records. Therefore, a *selfjoin* is needed:

```
select fst.x, lst.y
from Intervals fst, Intervals lst
where fst.x < lst.y
and …
```

Figure 1.7 - *Endpoints of the covering interval are constructed from the endpoints of the first and last intervals in a chain of intervals with no gaps.*

Next, the "no gaps" condition is introduced. Consider any interval endpoint between *fst.x* and *fst.y*. It has to be covered by some interval!

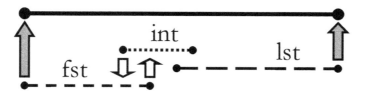

Figure 1.8 - *In the chain of intervals fst, int, lst the endpoint int.x is covered by the fst interval. Likewise, the fst.y is covered by the int.*

Actually, if there is a gap in a chain of intervals, then both ends of the gaps would be exposed (that is not covered by other intervals). This observation allows a small optimization, so that only the x endpoints will need checked.

Unfortunately, the "no gaps" condition cannot be naturally translated into SQL, since it does not support *universal quantifiers*. The standard approach is converting the clause into existential quantifiers, which will be explained in more detail in the section on Relational Division. Here let's take a little jump and write the whole condition at once:

```
select fst.x, lst.y
from Intervals fst, Intervals lst
where fst.x < lst.y
and not exists (
   select * from Intervals int
   where int.x > fst.x and int.x < lst.y
   and not exists (
      select * from Intervals cov
      where int.x >= cov.x and int.x =< cov.y
   )
) and …
```

That's not all. The chain of intervals has to be *maximal*, in other words, it cannot be extended at the either end.

Figure 1.9 - *The chain starting with the fst interval and ending with lst is not maximal, since the lst.y is covered by some other interval.*

This condition translates into one extra subquery:

```
select fst.x, lst.y
from Intervals fst, Intervals lst
where fst.x < lst.y
and not exists (
   select * from Intervals int
   where int.x > fst.x and int.x < lst.y
   and not exists (
      select * from Intervals cov
      where int.x >= cov.x and int.x =< cov.y
   )
) and not exists (
   select * from Intervals cov
   where cov.x < fst.x and fst.x <= cov.y
      or cov.x <= lst.y and lst.y < cov.y
)
```

The final query is surprisingly verbose. Terser expression would involve converting NOT EXISTS subqueries into counting.

Is (NOT) EXISTS or (NOT) IN faster?

This is the wrong question. The EXISTS and IN subqueries are equivalent; in fact, the optimizer uses the term *semijoin* for both. The NOT EXISTS and NOT IN subqueries are different as far as $NULL$ semantics is concerned, but still they are very similar so that the SQL execution engine uses the term *antijoin* for both. It might be argued that SQL standard should have defined them identically, leaving explicit control of $NULL$ semantics to the end user (by means of $IS\ (NOT)\ NULL$ predicate). History proved any attempt to get $UNKNOWN$ value semantics right as futile, therefore it is better just to forget about $NULL$s and aim for elementary consistency.

Which NOT EXISTS clause should be used, since two are available? Let's revisit both conditions:

- A chain of intervals must have no gaps (Figure 1.8)

- A chain is maximal if it has uncovered ends (Figure 1.9)

These conditions are not entirely independent, since every maximal chain of intervals is delimited by gaps on both ends. A change of perspective is needed.

Consider any pair of intervals *fst* and *lst*. Suppose *fst.x* and *lst.y* are not covered by other intervals. Are *fst* and *lst* the beginning and the end of a chain? Not necessarily, because there might be gaps between them. Let's shift our focus onto a set of *fst*, *lst* pairs such that *fst.x* and *lst.y* are not covered by other intervals. If there is a gap between some pair of intervals *fst1*, *lst1*, then it follows that there has to be another pair *fst2*, *lst2* with the same first element *fst2* = *fst1* and some other second element *lst2* such that *lst1.y* < *lst2.y*

Figure 1.10 - *A chain of intervals beginning with fst_1 and ending with lst_1 has a gap. Therefore, there is an element lst_2, such that $lst_2.y$ is not covered by any other interval.*

In other words, among all the *fst*, *lst* pairs with the same *fst* element, it is the pair with the minimal *lst* element that defines a chain without gaps.

Let's formalize these ideas. A NOT EXISTS subquery has already been written that defined a set of *fst*, *lst* pairs such that *fst.x* and *lst.y* are not covered by other intervals. Alternatively, the conditional summation pattern could have been applied. Indeed

```
select fst.x, lst.y, sum(
      case when cover.x < fst.x and fst.x <= cover.y
            or cover.x <= lst.y and lst.y < cover.y
            then 1 else 0 end
)
from intervals fst, intervals lst, intervals cover
where fst.y <= lst.y
group by fst.x, lst.y
```

counts if either *fst.x* or *lst.y* is covered by some interval. If the count is 0, then the *fst*, *lst* pair defines a maximal chain (possibly with gaps). Therefore, a formal query returning all the maximal chains is:

```
select fst.x, lst.y
from intervals fst, intervals lst, intervals cover
where fst.y <= lst.y
group by fst.x, lst.y
having sum(
      case when cover.x < fst.x and fst.x <= cover.y
            or cover.x <= lst.y and lst.y < cover.y
            then 1 else 0 end
) = 0
```

The final step is selecting all the pairs with the minimal *lst* element. All the pairs with the fixed *fst* element, which translates into *group by* are being considered:

```
select x, min(y) from (
   select fst.x, lst.y
   from intervals fst, intervals lst, intervals cover
   where fst.y <= lst.y
   group by fst.x, lst.y
   having sum(
         case when cover.x < fst.x and fst.x <= cover.y
               or cover.x <= lst.y and lst.y < cover.y
               then 1 else 0 end
   ) = 0
)
group by x
```

There is an important special case of the interval coalesce problem:

Given a set of integers, partition them into ranges of successive numbers.

This problem can also be called *interval packing*, and is the reverse of the *discrete interval sampling*, that will be studied in the next chapter.

Figure 1.11 - *Interval Packing. A set of integers 0,1,2,3,5,6,7,9 is packed into the intervals [0,3], [5,7], and [9,9].*

If each integer x is represented as a (closed) interval [x,x+1], then the problem reduces to interval coalesce. Rod West suggested a much more elegant solution[17], however. His key insight was an expression that groups the numbers within the same range. Then, if we know how to group integers, the ranges are defined by taking minimum and maximum inside each group. What criterion identifies each group?

It was shown in the section on counting how to enumerate rows in the increasing order:

```
select t.x, count(*) seq#
from T t, T tt
where tt.x <= t.x
group by t.x
```

It is the x - *seq#* expression that remains constant within each group!

---

[17] Perhaps, I'm little unfair by giving credits to people mostly from oracle community in this book. Unfortunately, the "big 3" database communities have grown apart, so that the same problem solution is rediscovered by different people. Joe Celko, who apparently lives in SQL Server world, gives the credit for a similar problem to Steve Kaas.

The rest is straightforward. We *group by* this expression and calculate *min* and *max* aggregate values, which are demarcating the beginning and the end of each interval:

```
select min(x), max(x) from (
   select x, rank() over(order by x) seq# from T
) group by x-seq
```

Predictably, this problem might occur in a slightly more complicated context. Our input relation can have one more column, say *name*, so that integers are grouped by the *name* values. Rod's solution scales up naturally to the new requirements. The additional grouping column just emerges in the appropriate places:

```
select name, min(x), max(x) from (
   select x, rank() over(partition by name order by x) seq#
   from T
) group by name, x-seq
```

Summary

- A (naturally ordered) list of values can be enumerated via join and grouping with aggregation, or SQL analytics query.

- Use the *CASE* operator inside the *SUM* aggregate function for counting. Leveraging the *CASE* operator is a pragmatic alternative to counting with Indicator and Step functions.

- Write complex queries as a chain of inner views nested inside each other.

- The DISTINCT operator can be expressed via *GROUP BY*.

- The *COUNT* operator does not have any arguments.

- The *GROUP BY* operator summarizes over two tables.

- Use the comma join syntax where possible.

Exercises

Exercise 1:

Suppose there are two queries:

```
select deptno, count(*) from emp;
select deptno, count(*) from emp
where sal < 1000;
```

Can they be combined into one?

Exercise 2:

The query

```
select count(distinct ename), count(*) from emp
```

refers to the *count* function, which accepts a funny argument with the *distinct* keyword.

Rewrite the query in such a way that it would utilize only the "politically correct" aggregate function – the *count(*)* with no arguments.

Exercise 3:

With column expression as an argument for the count() function and all NULL values are ignored, write an equivalent query for

```
select count(comm) from emp
```

via conditional summation.

Exercise 4:

There is no shorthand syntax for counting distinct column combinations. Write down a query that counts the distinct number of the *first_name, last_name* in the *Customers* table by separating *counting* and *distinction* in different query blocks.

Exercise 5:

The *having* clause is redundant. Transform

```
select deptno from emp
group by deptno
having min(sal) < 1000
```

into an equivalent form leveraging the inner subquery.

Exercise 6:

The correlated scalar subquery can be used within the *order by* clause. Explain the purpose of the following query:

```
select * from emp
order by (select dname from dept where emp.deptno=dept.deptno);
```

Exercise 7:

Express the indicator function 1_x via standard numeric functions *abs(x)* and *sign(x)*.

Exercise 8:

Figure 1.9 demonstrates one way to implement the maximal chain of intervals condition. Alternatively, the maximal chain could be defined as the one that maximizes the distance *lst.y − fst.x*. Write the query that formalizes that idea.

Exercise 9:

Write a set intersection query. Given a collection of sets, e.g.

```
set1 = {1,3,5,7,9}
set2 = {1,2,3,4,5}
```

```
set3 = {4,5,6,7}
```

stored as a relation *Sets:*

ID	ELEMENT
1	1
1	3
1	5
1	7
1	9
2	1
2	2
2	3
2	4
2	5
3	4
3	5
3	6
3	7

Your query should return the intersection of all the sets listed in the relation *Sets*; i.e. {5} in our example. Hint: group by the *element* column and count.

Exercise 10:

Counting words. Suppose you have a table of sentences

```
table Sentences {
    text  varchar(4000);
}
```

The SQL function *instr(string, substring, startPosition)* returns the position of the first occurrence of the *substring* in the *string* beginning with *startPosition*. Write a SQL query that counts the number of sentences where a given word is occurring once, twice, and so on.

Exercise 11:

This is an example[18] where nothing more than correct identification of a problem is required. Write a query which tells when an *id* has been a certain value for *x* consecutive years. Given the following table

ID	YR	VALUE
100	1998	0
100	1999	0
100	2000	0
100	2001	0
100	2002	1
100	2003	0
100	2004	0
100	2005	0
100	2006	0
100	2007	0
100	2008	1
200	1999	0
200	2001	0
200	2002	1
300	2001	0
300	2002	0
300	2003	0

find *id, startdate, enddate* when value is *0* for *3* or more consecutive years. The expected output is:

ID	STARTDATE	ENDDATE	YEARS
100	1998	2001	4
100	2003	2007	5
300	2001	2005	5

---

[18] Adopted from microsoft.public.sqlserver.programming

Integer Generators in SQL

Introduction

Counting as was introduced in Chapter 1 is fundamental to our culture. Some SQL queries however require more sophistication than simply counting rows. Although sometimes there is no obvious candidate relation to count, a need may arise requiring the generation of an arbitrary number of rows and the counting of those rows. Formally, what is needed is the *Integers* relation which contains nothing more than a single numeric column with a list of positive integer numbers.

Surprisingly, there is no built-in *Integers* relation in SQL[19]. The first half of this chapter will show about a dozen ways to cook it. And the second part of this chapter will introduce the numerous applications.

Integers Relation

Commercial databases do not come already equipped with the *Integers* relation. However, it is fairly easy to manufacture. Since the solution differs between various vendors, now is a good time to branch out this information.

Recursive With

DB2 has, arguably, the most satisfactory answer with *recursive* SQL:

---

[19] PostgreSQL user would probably smile and point out that there actually is a function `generate_series` that produces such a relation.

```
with Integers (num) as
( values(1)
  union all
  select num+1 from Integers
  where num < 100
)
select * from Integers
```

The execution flow literally follows the formal description. The *Integers* relation is defined via itself, hence the adjective "recursive". Unlike other relational operators, which determine the result instantaneously and by purely logical means, the recursive definition works in steps. The process begins with an empty *Integers* relation. Add to this, the first tuple *(num=1)*. After that is complete the recursive part

```
...
  select num+1 from Integers
  where num < 100
...
```

is ignited and starts producing additional tuples. The recursion stops as soon as the recursive part is unable to generate more tuples.

The only imperfection with this process is the hard-coded constant in the *where* condition. Was the *Integers* relation really defined or just the *IntegersThatAreLessThan100*? With this question in mind, it becomes very tempting to move the whole condition to the outer query block where it fits more naturally:

```
with Integers (num) as
( values(1)
  union all
  select num+1 from Integers
)
select * from Integers
where num < 100
```

Why this is such a good idea, and yet why it does not work will be a recurring theme in this chapter.

DB2 has enjoyed the recursive SQL feature for quite a while. This solution applies to Microsoft SQL Server circa 2005 as well. A reader interested in prior art is advised to lookup Usenet Groups history on Google, since the question, *"What is the analog of rownum in a MS Server?"* was asked and, perhaps, is still being asked about every week on the Microsoft SQL Server programming forum.

Big Table

There is about dozen of different ways to generate integers in Oracle. Moreover, every new release increases this number. The oldest and the least sophisticated method just hangs on the *rownum* column to some big table; the *all_objects* dictionary view being the most popular choice:

```
select rownum from all_objects where rownum < 100
```

The *rownum* is a pseudo column that assigns incremental integer values to the rows in the result set. This column name is Oracle proprietary syntax, hence the question from users of the other RDBMS platforms highlighted in the previous section.

The ROWNUM Pseudocolumn

The ROWNUM is a hack. Expression with a ROWNUM in a *where* clause

```
select ename

from Emp

where ROWNUM = 2
```

is responsible for an output that confuses a newbie.

ROWNUM predates the much more cleanly defined *row_number()* analytic function. For example

```
select ename, row_number() over (order by ename) num

from Emp
```

projects the *Emp* relation to the *ename* column, and extends it with an additional integer counter column. This extension, however, conflicts with the selection operator. Both

```
select ename, row_number() over (order by ename) num

from Emp

where num = 2
```

and

```
select ename, row_number() over (order by ename) num

from Emp

where row_number() over (order by ename) = 2
```

are illegal.

The *all_objects* view is fairly complicated, though. From a performance perspective, the *sys.obj$* dictionary table is a much better choice, because it is an actual table rather than a view.

Table Function

Either way, the previous solution looks ridiculous to anybody with little programming background. Integers can be easily created on the fly, so why does one have to refer to some stored relation let alone a view over several tables? The idea of relations which can be manufactured with code as opposed to stored relations leads to the concept of *Table Function*.

A table function is a piece of procedural code that can produce a result which can be understood by the SQL engine -- that is, a relation! A table function can have a parameter, so that the output relation depends on it. For all practical purposes it looks like a *Parameterized* view, and it is even called this in the SQL Server world. The *Integers* view is naturally parameterized with an upper bound value.

The table function concept evolved further to embrace the idea of *pipelining*. From a logical perspective, pipelining does not change anything: the table function output is still a relation. The function, however, does not require materializing the whole relation at once; it supplies rows one by one along with the consumer's demand. This implementation difference, however, has a significant implication in our case. The *integers* relation is infinite! By no means can one hope to materialize it in all entirety, hence the upper bound parameter in a non-pipelined version mentioned in the previous paragraph.

The size of the pipelined table function output does not necessarily have to be controlled by purely logical means. A row's producer (table function) is in an intricate relationship with a row's consumer (the enclosing SQL query), and there is a way for the consumer to tell the producer to stop.

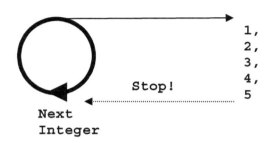

Figure 2.1 - *A producer generates integers in an infinite loop. As soon as an integer is built, it is shipped to a consumer. After digesting 5 integers the consumer decides that it had enough.*

Let's write such table function producing an infinite list of integers and see what happens:

```
CREATE TYPE IntSet AS TABLE OF Integer;

CREATE or replace FUNCTION Integers
  RETURN  IntSet PIPELINED IS
BEGIN
    loop
        PIPE ROW(0);
    end loop;
END;
/
```

Each table function is required to define the shape of the output it produces as an object type. We declared *IntSet* as a list of integers. The function implementation is unbelievably simple: the flow of control enters an infinite loop, where it creates a new output row during each iteration. Since the function is capable of producing a list of 0s only, it is calling the SQL query's responsibility to have a pseudo column expression that assigns integers incrementally. Alternatively, we could have a slightly more verbose *Integers* table function with a counter variable incremented during each loop iteration which pipes that integer to the output.

How is the *Integers* table function used? Simply use:

```
select rownum from Table(Integers)
```

Be careful though, a typical client programmatic interface allows opening a cursor and fetching the result set row by row. Normally, the client would stop when it exhausts the result set. In this case, the result set is infinite, so the client has to decide by itself when to stop. Of course, the decision when to stop can be moved to the server side and made explicit such as:

```
select rownum from Table(Integers)
where rownum < 1000
```

When designing a pipelined Integers function a rather popular alternative was neglected. Many would find it natural for the Integers function to have an argument specifying an upper limit in the range of generated integers. For example, Integers(5) returns the list 1,2,3,4,5; and the last could be reformulated in terms of this new function without the predicate:

```
select rownum from Table(Integers(1000))
```

Which style is better? Suppose somebody unfamiliar with the Integers function implementation asks:

What is the maximum number in the list of integers produced by this query?

Predicate *rownum <= 1000* gives the answer to the question immediately. While with the function parameter it might be *1000*, *999*, or even *21000* – it is impossible to tell for sure without examining the *Integers* function implementation.

Integers Relation

The case when one would need raw or only a slightly cooked list of
integers is relatively simple. If the *integers* relation is a part of a more
complex query, it would require a more elaborate analysis to decide
whether the query would terminate without an explicit server-side stop
condition.

Cube

One more approach leverages the *cube* operator:

```
select rownum from (
    select 0
    from dual
    group by cube(1,1,1,1,1)
)
```

This solution had drawn the following eloquent comment from a reader
named Mikito Harakiri:

*Most posters here[20] seem to have trouble seeing the difference between finite and
infinite.*

*OK, exponentiate the number, it is still produces a finite number (of rows). One day
your program with this "cool" cube solution would break just because you have been
lazy enough to code a trivial pipelined function. Essentially, cube is as bad as selecting*

_____

[20] Ask Tom forum, the thread "*how to display selective record twice in the query?*"

from obj$ (OK, col$ is probably bigger). Well, except that you take your fellow programmer's time, who has to understand your code. What is the purpose of this group by cube, in general, and why there are 5 parameters (and, say, not 6), in particular.

Table function method

```
select rownum from Table(Integers()) where rownum < 50
```

is much cleaner and robust.

Hierarchical Query

I have mentioned already DB2 integer generator leveraging recursive SQL. Oracle does not have recursive SQL capabilities at the time of this writing, so users have to use a non-standard hierarchical query extension. A contrast between Oracle and DB2 solutions is often enlightening. One fundamental difference between these two platforms is that Oracle seems to be able to detect loops, while DB2 does not make such a claim. Detecting loops in general is undecideable, which is the basis for DB2's position. Does Oracle's loop detection work because hierarchical extension has narrowed query expression capabilities compared to recursive SQL? Can this be challenged?

Consider the following typical hierarchical query:

```
select ename from emp
connect by empno = prior mgr
start with empno = 1000
```

First, Oracle finds all the nodes in the graph satisfying the *start with* condition. Then, for each batch of nodes found on a previous step, it finds a batch of extra nodes that satisfy the *connect by* condition. Any time the new node collides with the nodes that have been already discovered, it signals the *connect by* loop error. How does it identify the nodes? Should it compare all the relation attributes, or only those in the *select* clause or choose some other ones?

Integers Relation

It is easy to see that the attributes in the *select* clause should not matter. Indeed, adding a *rownum* pseudo column would artificially make the next node always appear different from its predecessors. The loop, however, is a property of the graph. Graph either has a cycle or it does not no matter what node labels exist. Therefore, the only columns which should be relevant for loop detection are the ones in the predicate with the *prior* prefix.

What hierarchical query is written without the *prior*? This experiment reveals a remarkably succinct integer generator:

```
select rownum from dual
connect by 0=0
```

As an alternative to the *rownum* pseudo column, *level* could be used:

```
select level from dual
connect by 0=0
```

Both queries produce an infinite result set. It is pipelined, however, so that the execution can be stopped either on the client or explicitly on the server:

```
select level from dual
connect by level < 100
```

Now that we have an ample supply of integer generators, we can proceed with applications.

String Decomposition

Given a relation A with a single column LST

LST
1,3,7

the query should output a relation with tuples containing individual substrings that are "separated by commas" in the original strings:

```
PREF
1
3
7
```

The clause "separated by commas" is decorated with quotation marks on purpose. While the value 3 is indeed enclosed with commas on both sides, 1 and 7 are delimited from one side only.

To convert this informal requirement into a formal language, the first thing to do is fix this nuisance. It is quite easy to accomplish using:

```
select ','||LST||',' LST from A
```

```
LST
,1,3,7,
```

Now, each value is enclosed from both sides. The answer is a substring between *n-th* and *n+1-th* delimiter position. Getting a little bit ahead of myself, I'll mention that a very elegant recursive SQL solution awaits us later. The following is one of Oracle's integer number generators:

```
with B as (select ','||LST||',' LST from A)
select substr(LST,instr(LST,',',1,num)+1,
              instr(LST,',',1,num+1)-instr(LST,',',1,num)-1) PREF
from B,(
  select rownum num from dual connect by rownum < 10
)
```

PREF
1
3
7

With this solution, it is instructive to reflect back and notice that without the additional commas in the beginning and at the end of the string the solution would be quite messy. Separate cases would have to be made for the values that are delimited from one side only. In one word, *rigorous* means *simple*!

Why does the query insist on producing exactly 9 integers? Well, 9 is a "reasonably big" number. Any number greater or equal to LENGTH(LST) would do. If we have more than one row in the original relation A, then we could simply take a maximum of the string lengths.

What about those rows with NULLs? Easy: anything unwanted could be filtered out with a proper predicate.

Admittedly, the last two answers taste like kludges. The solution feels even less satisfying if it is compared with the recursive SQL solution, which I promised before:

```
with decomposed( pref, post ) as (
  select  '',  lst from A
  union
  select substr(lst, 1, instr(lst,',')),
         substr(lst, instr(lst,',')+1, length(lst)) from decomposed
) select pref from decomposed where pref <> ''
```

The execution steps can be easily visualized:

Execution Step	Relation		New Tuples	
0	Pref	Post	Pref	Post
		1,3,7	1	3,7
1	Pref	Post	Pref	Post
		1,3,7	3	7
	1	3,7		
2	Pref	Post		
		1,3,7	Pref	Post
	1	3,7	7	
	3	7		
3	Pref	Post	Pref	Post
		1,3,7		
	1	3,7		
	3	7		
	7			

Interestingly, no longer is it required to decorate strings with a starting and trailing delimiter.

If your RDBMS of choice supports table functions, you might argue that the task of string parsing could be delegated to some procedural code. Here is implementation in Oracle posted on the OTN SQL& PL/SQL forum by Scott Swank:

```
CREATE TYPE Strings AS TABLE OF varchar2(100);

FUNCTION parse (
    text        IN   VARCHAR2,
    delimiter   IN   VARCHAR2 DEFAULT ',')
    RETURN Strings
  IS
    delim_len    CONSTANT PLS_INTEGER       := LENGTH (delimiter);
    tokens                 Strings    := Strings ();
    text_to_split          VARCHAR2 (32767);
    delim_pos              PLS_INTEGER;
  BEGIN
    tokens.DELETE;
    text_to_split := text;

    WHILE text_to_split IS NOT NULL
    LOOP
      delim_pos := INSTR (text_to_split, delimiter);

      IF delim_pos > 0
      THEN
        tokens.EXTEND;
        tokens (tokens.LAST) :=
                  SUBSTR (text_to_split, 1, delim_pos - 1);
        text_to_split :=
                  SUBSTR (text_to_split, delim_pos + delim_len);
      ELSE
        tokens.EXTEND;
        tokens (tokens.LAST) := text_to_split;
        text_to_split := NULL;
      END IF;
    END LOOP;

    RETURN tokens;
END parse;
```

Even though the implementation looks complicated, all that is visible from the SQL query is a function call:

```
select column_value
from table(parse('1,2,3,4'));
```

It might not seem obvious how to call this table function in a context where the input data is a set of strings. A *table* expression cannot be placed inside some subquery within the *select* or *where* clause, since it returns multiple rows[21]. The only solution is keeping it inside the *where* clause, although the function parameter has to be correlated with the source table:

---

[21] Unless we expand our scope to a **nested** tables.

SQL Design Patterns

```
create table sources (
   num integer,
   src varchar2(1000)
);

insert into sources values(1, '1.2.3,4.5,6,7');
insert into sources values(2, '8,9');

select    num,    t.*
from sources, table(parse(src)) t;
```

This syntax is reminiscent of ANSI SQL lateral views, where the second table expression is allowed to refer to the first one. From a theoretical perspective an expression with a lateral view is an asymmetric join with the join condition pushed inside the second table. This solution scales up nicely. For example we can parse a comma separated list, first and then parse the result once more

```
select    num,
   t1.column_value a,
   t2.column_value b
from sources t, table(parse(src)) t1,
table(parse(column_value,'.')) t2;
```

NUM	A	B
1	1.2.3	1
1	1.2.3	2
1	1.2.3	3
1	4.5	4
1	4.5	5
1	6	6
1	7	7
2	8	8
2	9	9

Enumerating Pairs

Enumerating pairs seems easy. Just build a Cartesian product of the two *integers* relations:

```
select i1.num x, i2.num y
from Integers i1, Integers i2
```

With a finite *integers* relation bounded by an arbitrary upper limit, there should not be any surprises. What if it is infinite, is it possible to drop the limit predicate on the server side and leverage the pipelining idea?

Pipelined Operators

When executing an SQL statement, the RDBMS engine represents it internally as a tree of *operators*. Each operator performs a relatively simple task; the complexity lies in the way the operators are combined together.

Each operator works as a black box. It consumes a relation as an input, massages it, and outputs the result to the other operator. If the operator is able to start outputting rows as soon as it consumed one or several rows, it is called *pipelined*. Pipelined operators do not block the execution flow; whereas *blocking* operators have to consume the whole input relation before outputting even a single row.

At first, the answer seems to depend on a join method employed by the SQL execution engine for this particular query. Both hash join and sorted merge join materialize their argument relations, therefore the execution plan involving any of those methods is never pipelined.

Nested loops are typically a pipelined method. It iterates via the outer relation, and for each row finds matching rows from the inner relation. In case of the Cartesian product of Integer relations, however, all the rows from the inner relation match and there are an infinite number of them! Therefore, the execution would be stuck scanning the inner table, and would never be able to get past the first row in the outer table. In other words, the nested loop join fails to deliver pipelined set of integer pairs as well.

SQL Design Patterns

Let's approach the problem from another angle. When a mathematician says "enumerating" she really means a one-to-one[22] mapping some set of objects into the integers. Figure 2.2 shows a nearly ubiquitous mapping of integer pairs into integers.

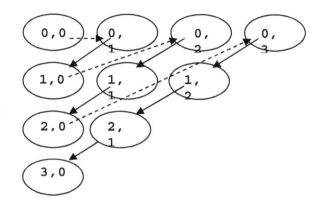

Figure 2.2 - *Enumerating all the pairs of integers. Each pair is assigned an integer which is the length of path to the origin. The origin (0,0) is mapped into 0, (0,1) is mapped into 1, and so on.*

Without further ado, here are the formulas for the *(x,y) -> n* mapping

$$n := \frac{1}{2}(x + y)(x + y + 1) + y$$

and the reverse *n -> (x,y)* mapping

[22] bijective

$$XplusY := \text{floor}\left(\frac{\sqrt{8\,n+1}\,-1}{2}\right)$$

$$x := n - \frac{(XplusY+1)\,XplusY}{2}$$

$$y := XplusY - x$$

Proving these formulas is left as an exercise for curious reader. Translating the above formulas into SQL is straightforward:

```
select n,n-(xplusy+1)*xplusy/2 x,
  xplusy-n+(xplusy+1)*xplusy/2 y
from (
  select FLOOR((SQRT(8*(rownum-1)+1)-1)/2) xplusy,
  rownum-1 n from dual connect by 1=1
)
```

N	X	Y
0	0	0
1	0	1
2	1	0
3	0	2
4	1	1
5	2	0
6	0	3
7	1	2
8	2	1
9	3	0
...	...	...

Even though the implementation side varies from vendor to vendor, it is instructive to see the execution statistics:

OPERATION	OUTPUT ROWS
⊟◖ VIEW	10
⊟◖ COUNT	10
⊟◖ CONNECT BY	10
⊟◖ FAST DUAL	1

Ignoring fancy operator names in the execution statistics above will show that the very first operator produces one row. This row performs a basis for the *connect by* iteration that starts producing rows one-by-one. Each row is pipelined through two more levels of processing to the top. The client receives each row[23], and after getting the tenth row, loses any interest in continuing further. The execution statistics is a snapshot at that moment.

Admittedly, using the above pipelined integer pairs implementation inside other queries as an inner view or subquery would only raise eyebrows. Those square root expressions are better be hidden behind a named view:

```
create view IntegerPairs as
select n,n-(xplusy+1)*xplusy/2 x,
  xplusy-n+(xplusy+1)*xplusy/2 y
from (
  select FLOOR((SQRT(8*(rownum-1)+1)-1)/2) xplusy,
  rownum-1 n from dual connect by 1=1
)
```

Was anything achieved with this pipelining idea using integer pairs implementation? Consider the following query:

Find positive integers X and Y satisfying both x + y = 10 and x − y = 2 equations

---

[23] In reality, the SQL programming interface buffers the result set, and transmit rows in batches of certain size.

With the *IntegerPairs* view the solution is immediate:

```
select x,y from IntegerPairs
where x+y=10 and x-y=2
```

Would it actually work? A pair *x=6 and y=5* is the unique solution of the system of equations, but would the execution really stop after we have it in the result set? Even if the client is not interested in more than one row from the result set, it has no way to communicate this to the server. If the result set is buffered, then the server would continue producing more pairs, and never stop.

Ad-Hoc Constants

If pipelining doesn't really work for constraint problems with two integer variables, why mention it at all? In an alternative approach it would simply be written

```
select x,y from (

  select num x from Integers where num < 234

), (

  select num y from Integers where num < 567

) where x+y=10 and x-y=2
```

which produces the correct answer without any risk of getting stuck in the infinite loop. Much left is to be desired for the code clarity, however. Those "safety" constants are eyesore, and they have to be estimated in advance. The values that work for one problem, might not work for next problem. A cartoon description of pipelining would define it as a programming style that avoids magical constants.

Enumerating Sets of Integers

When enumerating integer sets every integer is mapped into a set of integers[24]. Representing an integer in a binary numbering system provides a natural way to implement such mapping. Formally, in

$$N = a_0 \, 2^0 + a_1 \, 2 + a_2 \, 2^2 + a_3 \, 2^3 + etc$$

each a_i is either 0 or 1. Then, the sequence $(a_0, a_1, a_2, a_3, \ldots)$ is a characteristic vector of a set: i is an element of the set whenever $a_i = 1$. For example, $10 = 2^1 + 2^3$ maps into $\{1,3\}$. Here is an integer set enumeration for up to N=10:

N	Integer Set
1	{0}
2	{1}
3	{0,1}
4	{2}
5	{0,2}
6	{1,2}
7	{0,1,2}
8	{3}
9	{0,3}
10	{1,3}

Unfortunately, this output cannot be produced in SQL, at least, not yet. Later, a study of composite data types and how multiple values are aggregated into strings and collections will be presented. For now, how to build a relation, "i is an element of set N" is shown:

---

[24] When speaking of bijective mapping between integers and integer sets it is common to assume that the sets are **finite**, which we quietly adopted.

N	i
1	0
2	1
3	0
3	1
4	2
5	0
5	2
6	1
6	2
7	0
7	1
7	2
8	3
9	0
9	3
10	1
10	3

The implementation is easy. Take the *IntegerPairs* relation and recruit the BITAND and POWER SQL functions to filter the unwanted pairs (N, *i*) pairs:

```
select y N, x i from IntegerPairs
where bitand(power(2,x),y)>0
```

Although the idea of pipelining was somewhat discredited in the previous section, it may be recovered for this purpose. We take an infinite stream of integer pairs, apply a filter with the $bitand(power(2,x),y)>0$ predicate and cut a finite segment of the result on the client. With a non-pipelined *IntegerPairs* implementation (via Cartesian product of *Integers* relations) the execution would hang in an infinite loop.

Discrete Interval Sampling

Perhaps the second most common problem that utilizes the *Integers* relation is *unpacking* the intervals[25], or leveraging the Signal Processing terminology *Discrete Interval Sampling*.

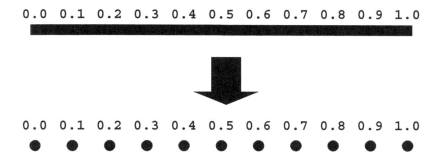

Figure 2.3 - *Discrete Interval Sampling example. Interval [0,1] is a continuum of points. We select 11 discrete points at the offset 0.1 each.*

Reduced to essentials the problem is the following. Given two dates, *'1-jan-2005'* and *'31-dec-2005'*, for example, return the list of the days in between. This is trivial, of course, if the *Dates* relation has already been filled in with the dates:

```
select day from Dates
where day between '1-jan-2005' and '31-dec-2005'
```

If the *Dates* relation is not present, why not simply manufacture it? All that is required is the support of the datetime/interval arithmetic by the RDBMS of your choice. Perhaps, the easiest approach is adding numeric

---

[25] C. J. Date, Hugh Darwen, and Nikos A. Lorentzos. Temporal Data and the Relational Model. 2003. Morgan Kaufmann.

values to the date represented in the *date* data type[26]. For example, adding 1 to today's date produces tomorrow's date. Likewise, *to_date('1-jan-2005')+1 is to_date('2-jan-2005')*, and so on. Therefore,

```
select to_date('1-jan-2005')+num
from Integers
where to_date('1-jan-2005')+num <= to_date('31-dec-2005')
```

will generate a list of days spanning the whole year. This toy query is frequently encountered as a part of more challenging puzzles.

Consider the following hotel reservation application. The *Bookings* table stores reservations made against a set of rooms:

RoomNo	"From"[27]	"To"	Customer
1	2005-05-07	2005-05-09	Jim
2	2005-05-08	2005-05-10	Steve
1	2005-05-11	2005-05-14	Bob

Users typically query what rooms are empty during a certain period. For example, querying all available rooms in the time period from 2005-05-07 to 2005-05-12 should return:

RoomNo	Day
2	2005-05-07
1	2005-05-10
2	2005-05-11
2	2005-05-12

We start with two relations: the first containing the list of all the rooms, and the second containing all the dates between 2005-05-07 and 2005-05-12. It is very tempting to define the first relation as

---

[26] The ANSI SQL equivalent to oracle's `date` is `timestamp` datatype.

[27] The "From" and "To" are SQL keywords, which is why they are decorated with quotation marks

```
select distinct RoomNo from Bookings
```

However, it is possible that a particular room is always empty, and therefore, has no records in the *Bookings* table. The whole *Bookings* table can be empty! Let's assume that we have the list of all rooms as one more relation -- the *Rooms* table. We are just one step from the solution. If a Cartesian product of the two relations is generated, the unwanted results (again, with scalar subquery) can be filtered out:

```
select RoomNo, Day
from (
    select to_date('07-May-2005')+num Day
    from Integers
    where to_date('07-May-2005')+num <= to_date('12-May-2005')
), Rooms r
where 0 = ( select count(*) from Bookings b
            where r.RoomNo = b.RoomNo
            and Day between "From" and "To"
);
```

Although the query has written itself effortlessly, much is left to be desired about its performance. A seasoned SQL performance analyst would immediately spot a couple of problems with this solution. Building a Cartesian product, first, and evaluating every resulting tuple with a subquery does not sound very promising. But the Cartesian product is unavoidable: if the *Bookings* relation is empty, then the result *must* be the Cartesian product. It is an interesting research question, whether one can reduce the cost associated with subquery evaluation in this example.

An alternative approach to the problem would reformulate the query from a business perspective.

- What is the list of rooms available during a certain interval?

- What is the average ratio of occupied rooms to empty rooms during a certain period?

Both of these queries can be answered without discrete interval sampling.

Summary

- Do not refer to any stored relation when generating integers.

- Recursive *with* integer generator is the cleanest solution.

- Integers provide a basis for more complex structures: integer pairs, sets of integers, etc.

- Integers are essential for iterative methods, e.g. String Decomposition, Discrete Interval Sampling.

Exercises

Exercise 1:

PostgreSQL has the *generate_series* function which has 3(!) arguments. Given *start*, *stop*, and *step* numbers it would produce a series of integers beginning with *start*, incremented by *step*, with the last element not exceeding the *stop*. Some controversial issues related to stop condition have already been explained. The *start* and *step*, however, are a much simpler matter. Prove that they are redundant.

Exercise 2:

In section "String Decomposition" can the pipelining idea be pushed forward, and the stop predicate *rownum < 10* be removed altogether? Try changing it to the *0 = 0* tautology and see what happens. Check up the execution plan, is it is pipelined? Try to influence the optimizer to use different join methods.

Exercise 3:

In the previous exercise, what if the condition filtering out unwanted NULLs is added? Could the execution possibly stop?

Exercise 4:

Can any of the integer generators that you studied in this chapter be abstracted into the *Integers* view with an infinite number of rows? What do you think is missing for a SQL engine to support such a view?

Exercise 5:

Derive the formulas for mapping integer pairs into integers.

Exercise 6:

Given a set of integers, for example

N
3
5

interpreted as the right interval boundaries, fill in each interval *[0,N]* with integers, for example:

N	i
3	1
3	2
3	3
5	1
5	2
5	3
5	4
5	5

Make sure the query is safe, in other words the auxiliary list of integers is bounded by the maximum integer from the original list.

Exercise 7:

Explain the following obfuscated query:

```
select -1/2+1/2*sqrt(1+8*sum(rownum)) from Emp
```

Exercise 8:

One way to check for balanced parenthesis across a string is to increment and decrement a running sum as each opening or closing parenthesis is encountered[28], for example:

```
(a or b) and (c or (d))
11111110000001111112210
```

Write a query that produces the running sum output:

Offset	Parenthesis Level
1	1
2	1
3	1
4	1
5	1
6	1
7	1
8	0
9	0
10	0
11	0
12	0
13	0
14	1
15	1
16	1
17	1

[28] Kendall Willets, private communications

18	1
19	1
20	2
21	2
22	1

Hint: apply a combination of techniques from Chapters 1 and 2. You need two integer generators: one for the offset, and one for conditional summation.

Exotic Operators in SQL

Introduction

The core of SQL language is fairly compact. Select-project-join, set operators, nested subqueries, inner views and aggregation all make up a very short but expressive list of operators. This is all that most users ever need for everyday usage. Once in a while, however, there comes a problem that cannot be solved by these means. Often, such a problem is evidence of a missing language feature.

User-defined aggregates and *Pivot*, which will be studied in the beginning of this chapter, are undoubtedly at the top of the list of desired features. *Symmetric Difference* and *Logarithmic Histograms* are two more query patterns that every developer sooner or later will encounter in their practice. And perhaps once in a lifetime this developer may come across either *Relational Division* or *Skyline*. Finally, the *Outer Union* is so rare that there is almost no chance an ordinary developer would ever need it. Yet, we'll get a chance to leverage it in the next chapter.

List Aggregate

List aggregate is not exactly a missing feature. It is implemented as a built-in operator in Sybase SQL Anywhere and MySQL. Given the original *Emp* relation

```
select deptno, ename from emp;
```

DEPTNO	ENAME
10	CLARK
10	KING
10	MILLER
20	ADAMS
20	FORD
20	JONES
20	SCOTT
20	SMITH
30	ALLEN
30	BLAKE
30	JAMES
30	MARTIN
30	TURNER
30	WARD

the query

```
select deptno, list(ename||', ')
from emp
group by deptno
```

is expected to return

DEPTNO	LIST(ename||', ')
10	CLARK, KING, MILLER
20	ADAMS, FORD, JONES, SCOTT, SMITH
30	ALLEN, BLAKE, JAMES, MARTIN, TURNER, WARD

The other vendors do not have a built-in *list* aggregate, but offer overwhelming functionality that allows implementing it easily. If your platform allows programming user-defined aggregate functions, simply search the code on the net, as it is most likely somebody has already written the required code. For Oracle the string aggregate function implementation named *stragg* may be easily found on the Ask Tom forum.

List Aggregate

Originally, SQL intended to be a "pure" declarative language. It had some built-in functions, but soon it was discovered that introducing User Defined Functions (UDF) makes the SQL engine *extensible*. Today, UDF is arguably one of the most abused features. In the industry, I have seen UDF with 200+ parameters wrapping a trivial insert statement, UDF used for query purposes, etc. Compare it to the integer generator UDF from Chapter 2, which was written only once and was intended to be used in numerous applications.

A User-defined aggregate is the standard way of implementing *list* aggregate. Let's explore alternative solutions. A recursive SQL does not miss an opportunity to demonstrate its power. The idea is to start with the empty list for each department and add records with the list incremented whenever the department has an employee name greater than last list increment. Among all the list of names, select those that have maximal length:

```
with emp_lists (deptno, list, postfix, length) as
( select distinct deptno, '', '', 0
from emp
  union all
  select e.deptno, list || ', ' || ename, ename, length+1
from emp_lists el, emp e
where el.deptno = e.deptno
and e.ename > el.postfix
)
select deptno, list from emp_lists e
where length = (select max(length)
                from emp_lists ee
                where e.deptno = ee.deptno)
```

Watch out for pitfalls. It is very tempting to start with the lexicographically minimal employee name per each department instead of the empty set. But this would not work for departments with zero employees.

The idea behind the recursive SQL solution carries over to the *connect by* solution:

```
with concat_enames as (
  select deptno, sys_connect_by_path(ename,',') aggr, level depth
  from emp e
  start with ename=(select min(ename) from emp ee
                    where e.deptno=ee.deptno)
  connect by ename > prior ename and deptno = prior deptno
) select deptno, aggr from concat_enames e
where depth=(select max(depth) from concat_enames ee
             where ee.deptno = e.deptno);
```

Next, there go various methods leveraging collections

```
CREATE or replace TYPE strings AS TABLE OF VARCHAR2(100);
/

CREATE or replace Function CONCAT_LIST ( lst IN strings )
  RETURN  VARCHAR2 AS
    ret    varchar2(1000);
BEGIN
    FOR j IN 1..lst.LAST  LOOP
        ret := ret || lst(j);
    END LOOP;
    RETURN ret;
END;
/

SELECT  deptno,
        CONCAT_LIST(
          CAST(MULTISET(
            SELECT ename||',' FROM EMP ee WHERE e.deptno=ee.deptno )
        AS strings)) empls
FROM    emp e
group by deptno;
```

including the one with a little bit cleaner syntax:

```
SELECT deptno,
       CONCAT_LIST(CAST( COLLECT(ename) AS strings )) empls
FROM    emp
group by deptno;
```

Another variation of the previous method leverages a function that accepts a cursor as an argument instead of a collection:

List Aggregate

```
CREATE or replace FUNCTION CONCAT_LIST( cur SYS_REFCURSOR )
  RETURN  VARCHAR2 IS
    ret VARCHAR2(32000);
    tmp VARCHAR2(4000);
BEGIN
    loop
        fetch cur into tmp;
        exit when cur%NOTFOUND;
            ret := ret || tmp;
    end loop;
    RETURN ret;
END;
/

select distinct
    deptno,
    CONCAT_LIST(CURSOR(
        select ename ||',' from emp ee where e.deptno = ee.deptno
    ) employees
from emp e;
```

Admittedly, the function concatenating values in a collection adds a little bit of a procedural taste. Again, such a general purpose function should not be exposed as a part of the solution at all. It is obvious that the CONCAT_LIST function should already be in the RDBMS library.

So far, half a dozen various aggregate string concatenation methods have been counted. And yet, not all of them are created equal from a performance perspective, of course. The most efficient solutions are the user-defined aggregation and the leveraging *collect* function. Do not hastily dismiss the rest, however. If nothing else, the problem of writing a *list* aggregate is still a great job interview question. A programmer's SQL skills (on the scale 0 to 6) can be rated by the number of different approaches that she can count.

Product

Product is another aggregate function, which is not on the list of built-in SQL functions. Randomly browsing any mathematical book however reveals that the product symbol occurs much less frequently than summation. Therefore, it is unlikely to expect the product to grow outside a very narrow niche. Yet there are at least two meaningful applications.

Factorial

If the product aggregate function were available, it would make the factorial calculation effortless:

```
select prod(num) from integers where num <=10  -- 10!
```

As always, a missing feature encourages people to become very inventive. From a math perspective, any multiplicative property can be translated into an additive one if the logarithm function is applied. Therefore, instead of multiplying numbers, their logarithms can be added, and the result exponentiated. The rewritten factorial query is still very succinct:

```
select exp(sum(ln(num))) from integers where num <=10
```

At this point most people realize that product via logarithms does not work in all the cases. The *ln* SQL function throws an exception for negative numbers and zero. After recognizing this fact, however, the problem could be fixed immediately with a *case* expression.

Numbers in SQL

If you feel uneasy about "fixing" an elegant *exp(sum(ln(…)))* expression with case analysis, it's an indicator that you as a programmer reached a certain maturity level. Normally, there are no problems when generalizing clean and simple concepts in math. What exactly is broken?

The problem is that the logarithm is a multivalued function defined on complex numbers. For example, $\ln(-1) = i\pi$ (taken on principal branch). Then, $e^{i\pi} = -1$ as expected!

Writing a function calculating factorial is perhaps one of the most ubiquitous exercises in procedural programming. It is primarily used to demonstrate the recursion. It is very tempting, therefore, to try recursive SQL:

```
with factorial (n, f) as (
   values(1, 1)
  union all
   select n+1, f*(n+1) from factorial
   where n<10
)
select * from factorial
```

Joe Celko suggested one more method - calculating factorial via Gamma function. A polynomial approximation with an error of less than $3*10^{-7}$ for $0 \leq x \leq 1$ is:

$$\Gamma(x+1) = 1 - 0.577191652\ x + 0.988205891\ x^2 - 0.897056937\ x^3 + 0.918206857 * x^4 - 0.756704078\ x^5 + 0.482199394\ x^6 - 0.193527818\ x^7 + 0.035868343\ x^8$$

Unfortunately, the error grows significantly outside of the interval $0 \leq x \leq 1$. For example,

$$\Gamma(6) = 59.589686421$$

Factorial alone could hardly be considered a convincing case for the product aggregate function. While factorial is undoubtedly a cute mathematical object, in practice it is never interesting to such an extent as to warrant a dedicated query. Most commonly, factorial occurs as a part of more complex expression or query, and its value could be calculated on the spot with an unglamorous procedural method.

Interpolation

Interpolation is more pragmatic justification for the product aggregate. Consider the following data:

X	Y
1	2
2	6
3	
4	8
5	
6	
7	6

Can you guess the missing values?

When this SQL puzzle was posted on the Oracle OTN forum, somebody immediately reacted suggesting the *lag* and *leading* analytic functions as a basis for calculating intermediate values by averaging them. The problem is that the number of intermediate values is not known in advance, so my first impression was that the solution should require leveraging recursion or a hierarchical SQL extension, at least. A breakthrough came from Gabe Romanescu, who posted the following analytic SQL solution:

```
select X,Y
       ,case when Y is null
        then yLeft+(rn-1)*(yRight-yLeft)/cnt
        else Y end /*as*/ interp_Y
from (
  select X, Y
       ,count(*) over (partition by grpa) cnt
       ,row_number() over (partition by grpa order by X) rn
       ,avg(Y) over (partition by grpa) yLeft
       ,avg(Y) over (partition by grpd) yRight
  from (
    select X, Y
           ,sum(case when Y is null then 0 else 1 end)
           over (order by X)    grpa
           ,sum(case when Y is null then 0 else 1 end)
           over (order by X desc) grpd
    from data
  )
);
```

As usual in case of complex queries with multiple levels of inner views, the best way to understand it is executing the query in small increments.

The inner-most query introduces two new columns, with the sole purpose to group spans with missing values together.

```
select X, Y
       ,sum(case when Y is null then 0 else 1 end)
       over (order by X)     grpa,
       ,sum(case when Y is null then 0 else 1 end)
       over (order by X desc) grpd
from data;
```

X	Y	GRPA	GRPD
1	2	1	4
2	6	2	3
3		2	2
4	8	3	2
5		3	1
6		3	1
7	6	4	1

The next step

```
select X, Y
       ,count(*) over (partition by grpa) cnt
       ,row_number() over (partition by grpa order by X) rn
       ,avg(Y) over (partition by grpa) yLeft
       ,avg(Y) over (partition by grpd) yRight
from (
    select X, Y
           ,sum(case when Y is null then 0 else 1 end)
           over (order by X)     grpa
           ,sum(case when Y is null then 0 else 1 end)
           over (order by X desc) grpd
    from data
)
```

X	Y	CNT	RN	YLEFT	YRIGHT
1	2	1	1	2	2
2	6	2	1	6	6
3		2	2	6	8
4	8	3	1	8	8
5		3	2	8	6
6		3	3	8	6
7	6	1	1	6	6

calculates four more columns:

- cnt – length of each span

- rn – offset inside the span

- yLeft – the Y value at the left boundary

- yRight – the Y value at the right boundary

The aggregate function – *avg* – is pretty arbitrary. There is only one non NULL value in each partition.

Now, everything is ready for the final step in which the linear interpolation formula is applied:

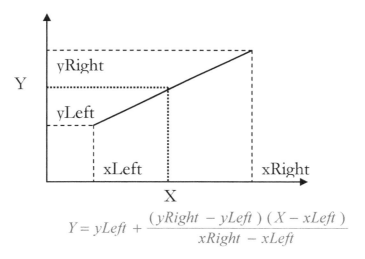

$$Y = yLeft + \frac{(yRight - yLeft)(X - xLeft)}{xRight - xLeft}$$

Figure 3.1 - *Linear interpolation formula calculates function value Y at the intermediate coordinate X.*

Note that instead of the xLeft and xRight variables we have cnt = xRight – xLeft and rn = X - xLeft.

A query leveraging an analytic SQL extension can be expressed in standard SQL:

```
select X, Y,
    (select min(bLeft.Y+( bRight.Y - bLeft.Y)*
            (bb.X- bLeft.X)/( bRight.X - bLeft.X) )
    from data bLeft, data bRight
    where bLeft.X < bRight.X
    and bLeft.Y is not null and bRight.Y is not null
    and not exists(select 0 from data bi
            where bLeft.X < X and X < bRight.X
            and bi.Y is not null)
    and bb.X between bLeft.X and bRight.X) /*as*/ interp_Y
from data bb
```

Arguably, this solution is more intuitive. The original relation can be scanned and an extra column added as a scalar subquery.

The original relation corresponds to point (X,Y) on the figure. In the subquery points (bLeft.X,bLeft.Y) and (bRight.X,bRight.Y) are the boundaries of the span that we are filling in with values. The *min* aggregate is bogus. It insures that the subquery in the *select* clause is scalar. Without aggregation the subquery returns either one value or two identical values.

What if the missing values are not bound with a known value at the end of the range? This can certainly be addressed as a special case and at the cost of making the query more complicated. Alternatively, this snag is nicely solved with *non-linear interpolation*, in general, and *Lagrange Interpolating Polynomial*, in particular

$$\sum_{j=1}^{n} y_j \left(\prod_{k=1}^{j-1} \frac{x - x_k}{x_j - x_k} \right) \left(\prod_{k=j+1}^{n} \frac{x - x_k}{x_j - x_k} \right)$$

Here is the product symbol, at last!

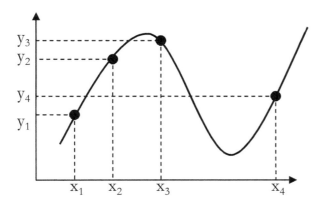

Figure 3.2 - *Lagrange interpolating polynomial is the most "natural" way to draw a curve through a number of points. Given 4 points (x_1, y_1), (x_2, y_2), (x_3, y_3), and (x_4, y_4), there is a unique cubic polynomial $a \cdot x^3 + b \cdot x^2 + c \cdot x + d$ that goes through all of them. It is Lagrange polynomial!*

Polynomial is a simpler concept than the piece-wise linear function. A cleaner concept translates into a simpler SQL, but the interpolation result is slightly different, of course.

```
select x, sum(y*mul) interp_Y from (
  select x,j,y, product(a) mul
  from (
    select bb.X x, bj.X j, bj.Y y, (bb.X-bk.X)/(bj.X-bk.X) a
    from data bj,data bk, data bb
    where bj.Y is not null and bk.Y is not null
    and bj.X!=bk.X
  ) group by x,j,y
) group by x
```

Pivot

Pivot and *Unpivot* are two fundamental operators that exchange rows and columns. Pivot aggregates a set of rows into a single row with additional columns. Informally, given the *Sales* relation,

Product	Month	Amount
Shorts	Jan	20
Shorts	Feb	30
Shorts	Mar	50
Jeans	Jan	25
Jeans	Feb	32
Jeans	Mar	37
T-shirt	Jan	10
T-shirt	Feb	15

the pivot operator transforms it into a relation with fewer rows, and some column headings changed:

Product	Jan	Feb	Mar
Shorts	20	30	50
Jeans	25	32	37
T-shirt	10	15	

Unpivot is informally defined as a reverse operator, which alters this relation back into the original one.

A reader who is already familiar with the Conditional Summation idiom from Chapter 1 would have no difficulty writing a pivot query in standard SQL:

```
select Product,
       sum(case when Month='Jan' then Amount else 0 end) Jan,
       sum(case when Month='Feb' then Amount else 0 end) Feb,
       sum(case when Month='Mar' then Amount else 0 end) Mar
from Sales
group by Product
```

Why aggregation and grouping? Aggregation is a natural way to handle data collision; when several values map to the same location. For example, a request made for the record of sales for the month of January results in two records appearing. The reason for this collision may be either an error in the input data or the result of a projection applied in the inner view. The original *Sales* relation might include the *Month* and *Day* columns, but the projection simply discarded the day information. Hence, summation is the right way to get the correct answer[29].

Unfortunately, the approach with the straightforward query above quickly shows its limitations. First, each column has a repetitive syntax which is impossible to factor in. More important, however, is the inability to accommodate a dynamic list of values. In this example, the (full) list of months is static, but change months to years, and we have a problem.

SQL Server 2005[30] introduced the pivot operator as syntax extension for a table expression in the *from* clause:

```
select * from
(Sales pivot (sum(Amount) for Month in ('Jan', 'Feb', 'Mar'))
```

As soon as a new feature is introduced people start wondering if it can accommodate more complex cases. For example, can two aggregations be performed at once? Given the *Sales* relation, can the sales total amounts be outputted together with sales counts like this?

---

[29] It may be argued that it is the projection that should have taken care of aggregation, while pivot should simply throw in an exception in case of data collision

[30] Conor Cunningham, Goetz Graefe, César A. Galindo-Legaria: PIVOT and UNPIVOT: Optimization and Execution Strategies in an RDBMS. VLDB 2004: 998-1009

Product	JanCnt	FebCnt	MarCnt	JanSum	FebSum	MarSum
Shorts	1	1	1	20	30	50
Jeans	1	1	1	25	32	37
T-shirt	1	1		10	15	

The column names had to be changed in order to accommodate extra columns, and if nothing else, the changed column names should hint the solution. The other idea, which should be immediately obvious from the way the table columns are arranged in the display, is that the result is a join between the two primitive pivot queries:

Product	JanCnt	FebCnt	MarCnt
Shorts	1	1	1
Jeans	1	1	1
T-shirt	1	1	

And

Product	JanSum	FebSum	MarSum
Shorts	20	30	50
Jeans	25	32	37
T-shirt	10	15	

Well, what about those fancy column names? There is nothing like *JanCnt* in the original data. Indeed there is not, but transforming the month column data into the new column with the *Cnt* postfix can be done easily with string concatenation. Therefore, the answer to the problem is:

```
select scount.*, ssum.* from (
select * from (
  (select product, month || 'Cnt', amount from Sales)
  pivot (count(*) for Month in ('JanCnt', 'FebCnt', 'MarCnt')
) scount, (
select * from (
  (select product, month || 'Sum', amount from Sales)
  pivot (sum(Amount) for Month in ('JanSum', 'FebSum', 'MarSum')
```

```
) ssum
where scount.product = ssum.product
```

When I posted this solution on the SQL server programming forum, Adam Machanic objected noting that is very inefficient compared to the conditional summation version:

```
select Product,
       sum(case when Month='Jan' then 1 else 0 end) JanCnt,
       sum(case when Month='Feb' then 1 else 0 end) FebCnt,
       sum(case when Month='Mar' then 1 else 0 end) MarCnt,
       sum(case when Month='Jan' then Amount else 0 end) JanSum,
       sum(case when Month='Feb' then Amount else 0 end) FebSum,
       sum(case when Month='Mar' then Amount else 0 end) MarSum
from Sales
group by Product
```

The culprit is the pivot clause syntax. It would have been a much more natural design if

- The pivot operator were designed as shorthand for the conditional summation query, and

- The pivot clause were allowed in a *select* list, rather than being a part of a table reference in the *from* clause.

The other popular request is pivot on multiple columns. Given the *Sales* relation extended with one extra column,

Product	Month	Day	Amount
Shorts	Jan	1	20
Shorts	Jan	2	30
Shorts	Jan	3	50
Jeans	Feb	1	25
Jeans	Feb	2	32
Jeans	Feb	3	37

pivot it over the combination of *Month* and *Day* columns.

This is much easier, simply concatenate the *Month* and the *Day* values and consider it as a pivot column:

```
select * from (
  (select product, month || '_' || day as Month_Day, amount
  from Sales)
  pivot (count(*) for Month_Day in ('Jan_1', 'Jan_2', 'Jan_3', …)
)
```

As this example demonstrates, the number of pivoted values easily becomes unwieldy, which warrants more syntactic enhancements.

Unpivot in a standard SQL syntax is:

```
select product, 'Jan' as Month, Jan as Amount from PivotedSales
 union all
select product, 'Feb' as Month, Feb as Amount from PivotedSales
 union all
select product, 'Mar' as Month, Mar as Amount from PivotedSales
```

Again it is repetitive and not dynamically extensible. In SQL Server 2005 syntax, it becomes:

```
select * from
(PivotedSales unpivot (Amount for Month in ('Jan', 'Feb', 'Mar'))
```

The introduction of *pivot* and *unpivot* operators in SQL opens interesting possibilities for data modeling. It may reincarnate the outcast Entity-Attribute-Value (EAV) approach. EAV employs a single "property table" containing just three columns: *propertyId*, *propertyName*, and *propertyValue*. The EAV styled schema design has a grave implication on how data in this form can (or rather cannot) be queried.

Even the simplest aggregate with *group by* queries cannot be expressed without implicitly transforming the data into a more appropriate view. Indexing is also problematic. Regular tables routinely have composite indexes, while the EAV table has to be self-joined or pivoted before even getting to a relation with more than one property value column. Pivot makes an EAV table look like a regular table.

Symmetric Difference

Suppose there are two tables A and B with the same columns, and you would like to know if there is any difference in their contents.

Relation Equality

A reader with an Object Oriented programming background might wonder why the Relational model in general, and SQL in particular, does not have an equality operator. You'd think the first operator you'd implement for a data type, especially a fundamental data type, would be equality! Simple: this operator is not relationally closed, as the result is Boolean value and not a relation.

The **Symmetric Difference** query provides a definitive answer:

```
(
 select * from A
 minus
 select * from B
) union all (
 select * from B
 minus
 select * from A
)
```

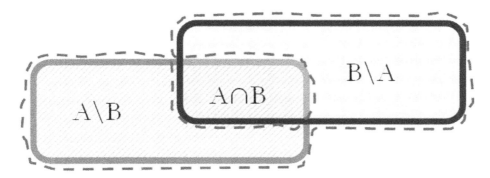

Figure 3.3 - *Symmetric difference of two sets A and B can be expressed as either $(A \setminus B) \cup (B \setminus A)$, or $(A \cup B) \setminus (A \cap B)$.*

In practice, however, this query is a sluggish performer. For my test I've created tables *A* and *B* with 100000 and 100010 rows correspondingly:

```
create table A as
select obj# id, name from sys.obj$
where rownum < 100000;

create table B as
select obj# id, name from sys.obj$
where rownum < 100010;
```

For such moderately sized tables the execution time about 2 sec is unacceptable. For comparison, it takes only 100 msec to scan an individual table *A* or *B*.

With a naïve evaluation strategy, the execution flow and the operators are derived verbatim from the SQL which has been written. First, each table has to be scanned twice. Then, four sort operators are applied in order to exclude duplicates. Next, the two set differences are computed, and finally, the two results are combined together with the union operator.

RDBMS implementations today, however, have pretty impressive query transformation capabilities. In our case, set difference can already be internally rewritten as *anti-join*. If not then, perhaps, the query optimizer can be influenced to transform the query into the desired form. Otherwise, has to be explicitly rewritten:

```
select * from A
where (col1,col2,…) not in (select col1,col2,… from B)
    union all
select * from B
where (col1,col2,…) not in (select col1,col2,… from A)
```

Duality between Set and Join Operators

For two tables A and B with the same columns, set intersection

select * from A

intersect

select * from B

can be expressed as a semi-join

select distinct * from A

where (col1,col2,...) in (select col1,col2,... from B)

Likewise, set difference

select * from A

intersect

select * from B

can be expressed as an anti-join

select distinct * from A

where (col1,col2,...) not in (select col1,col2,... from B)

Transforming set into join operators expands optimizer search space.
Optimizer could explore new, previously unavailable join order
permutations.

Unfortunately, transforming set operators into joins did not have any significant effect, at least in my experiment.

The symmetric difference can be expressed via aggregation:

```
select * from (
  select id, name,
    sum(case when src=1 then 1 else 0 end) cnt1,
    sum(case when src=2 then 1 else 0 end) cnt2
  from (
    select id, name, 1 src from A
    union all
    select id, name, 2 src from B
  )
  group by id, name
)
where cnt1 <> cnt2
```

This appeared to be a rather elegant solution[31] where each table has to be scanned only once, until it was discovered that it has about the same performance as the canonic symmetric difference query.

When comparing data in two tables there are actually two questions that one might want to ask:

- Is there any difference? The expected answer is Boolean.

- What are the rows that one table contains, and the other does not?

Question #1 can be answered faster than #2 with a hash value based technique.

The standard disclaimer of any hash-based technique is that it is theoretically possible to get a wrong result. The rhetorical question, however, is how often did the reader experience a problem due to hash value collision? I never did. Would a user be willing to accept a (rather negligible) risk of getting an incorrect result for a significant performance boost?

In a hash-based method each table is associated with a single aggregated hash value. This should be carried out in such a way that changing a single character or digit in any field must cause the aggregate value change. Aggregation via *min* and *max* functions wouldn't meet this requirement, while the *sum* would.

---

[31] suggested by Marco Stefanetti in an exchange at the Ask Tom forum

Here is one method to calculate the aggregated table value:

```
select sum( ora_hash(id||'|'||name, POWER(2,16)-1) )
from A
```

There all row fields[32] were concatenated, and the string translated into a hash value. Alternatively, hash values could have been calculated for each field, and some asymmetric function applied in order for the resulting hash value to be sensitive in respect to column permutations:

```
select 1 * sum( ora_hash(id,   POWER(2,16)-1) )
     + 2 * sum( ora_hash(name, POWER(2,16)-1) )
from A
```

Row hash values are added together with ordinary sum aggregate, but we could have written a modulo $2^{16}-1$ user-defined aggregate hash_sum in the spirit of the CRC (Cyclic Redundancy Check) technique.

Hash value calculation time is proportional to the table size. This is noticeably better than the symmetric difference query, where the bottleneck was in the sorting.

We can do even better, at the expense of introducing a materialized view. The hash value behaves like an aggregate, and therefore, can be calculated incrementally. If a row is added into a table, then a new hash value is a function of the old hash value and the added row. Incremental evaluation means good performance, and the comparison between the two scalar hash values is done momentarily.

Histograms in SQL

The concept of histograms originated in statistics. Admittedly, statistics never enjoyed the reputation of being the most exciting math subject. I never was able to overcome a presumably unfair impression that it is just

---

[32] with a dedicated " | " separator, in order to guarantee uniqueness

a collection of ad-hoc methods. Yet a typical database table has a huge volume of data, and histograms provide an opportunity to present it in compact human digestible report.

A histogram can be built on any (multi-)set of values. In the database world this set comes from a table column, so values can be numerical, character, or other datatypes. For purposes in this book, it is convenient to order the values and then index them as in Figure 3.4

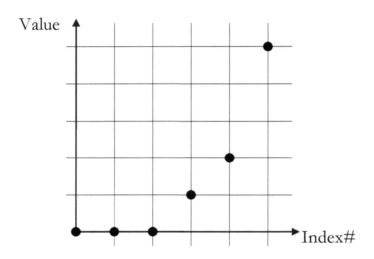

Figure 3.4 - *An example of multi-set {0,0,0,1,2,5} represented as an index function, which maps a set of indexes {0,1,2,3,4,5} into a set of values {0,1,2,5}.*

This might not feel natural at first, but the two dimensions on the graph provide an insight as to why there are exactly two kinds of histogram.

Equal-Width Histogram

Equal-width histogram partitions the graph horizontally, as shown on Figure 3.5.

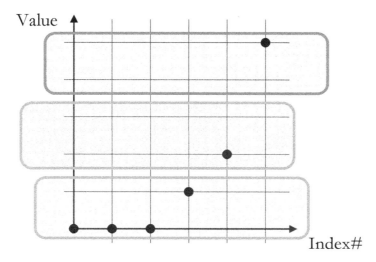

Figure 3.5 - *Equal-width histogram partitioned the set {0,1,2,5} of values into sets {1,2}, {3}, and {5}.*

Evidently, there is something wrong here, either with the term *equal-width histogram*, or my unorthodox interpretation. First, the partitioning is vertical; second, why do buckets have to be of uniform size? Well, if the coordinates are swapped in an attempt to make partitioning conform to its name, then it would not be a function anymore. Also, partitioning does not have to be uniform. Histograms with logarithmic partitioning will be studied later.

There is one special type of equal-width histogram – *frequency histogram*. It partitions the set of values in the finest possible way, Figure 3.6.

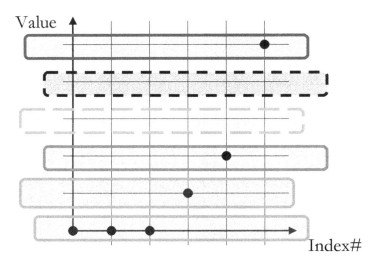

Figure 3.6 - *Frequency histogram is equal-width histogram with the finest possible partitioning of the value set.*

The two kinds of objects -- (indexed) values and buckets -- can now be associated in a query. Either of the following questions should be asked:

- what bucket a particular value falls in, or

- what is the aggregate value in each bucket (there may be interest in more than one aggregate function)

In the first case, the query returns one extra attribute per each record in the input data. Given the input set of data,

Index#	Value
0	0
1	0
2	0
3	1
4	2
5	5

the expected output is:

Index#	Value	Bucket
0	0	0
1	0	0
2	0	0
3	1	0
4	2	1
5	5	2

As suggested in Figure 3.4, the number in the *Bucket* column is determined by the *Value*.

Enough abstract talk, let's write some SQL queries.

Assign a bucket number to each record in the IndexedValues table. All the records with values in the range from 0 to 1 are placed into 0th bucket, values in the range 2 to 3 go into bucket number 1, etc.

The key to the solution is identifying what kind of function mapping of indexes into buckets satisfies the (informal) specification. The *floor(index#/2)* does, so the solution is as simple as:

```
select index#, value, floor(value/2) bucket
from IndexedValues
```

Often, the mapping from indexes to buckets is not determined by a mathematical function, like the combination of floor and division in the previous example. Consider:

Distribute IndexedValues records into 4 buckets. If total number of records is n, then all the records with values in the range from 0 to n/4 are placed into 0th bucket, values in the range n/4 to n/2 go into bucket number 1, etc.

This informal query translates 1-to-1 into SQL:

```
select index#, value, floor(4*value/n) bucket
from IndexedValues, (select count(*) n from IndexedValues)
```

Let's move on to the second type of queries – aggregates grouped by bucket.

Assign a bucket number to each record in the IndexedValues table. All the records with values in the range from 0 to 1 are placed into 0th bucket, values in the range 2 to 3 go into bucket number 1, etc. For each bucket count the number of values that fall into this bucket.

This version is just a small increment to the query written earlier:

```
select floor(value/2) bucket, count(*)
from IndexedValues
group by floor(value/2)
```

A simplified version of the previous query in verbose form defines a frequency histogram.

Assign a bucket number to each record in the IndexedValues table. The record with value 0 is placed into 0th bucket, value 1 goes into bucket number 1, etc. For each bucket count the number of values that fall into this bucket.

It is formally expressed as celebrated *group by* query:

```
select value bucket, count(*)
from IndexedValues
group by value
```

Equal-Height Histogram

Equal-height histogram partitions the graph vertically, as shown on Figure 3.7.

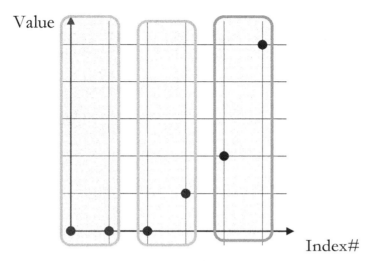

Figure 3.7 - *Equal-height histogram partitioned the set {0,1,2,3,4,5} of indexes into sets {0,1}, {2,3}, and {4,5}.*

The development in the rest of the section would mimic an equal-width case with the *value* and *index#* roles reversed. There is some asymmetry, though. Unlike the equal-width case where partitioning values with the finest granularity led to the introduction of the frequency histogram, there is nothing interesting about partitioning indexes to the extreme. Each bucket corresponds one-to-one to the index, so the concept of a bucket in no longer needed.

Let's proceed straight to queries. They require little thought other than the formal substitution of *value* by *index#*.

Assign a bucket number to each record in the IndexedValues table. All the records with indexes in the range from 0 to 1 are placed into 0th bucket, indexes in the range 2 to 3 go into bucket number 1, etc.

```
select index#, value, floor(index#/2) bucket
from IndexedValues
```

There is one subtlety for an aggregate query. The record count within each bucket is not interesting anymore, as in our example we know it's trivially 2. We might ask other aggregate functions, though:

Assign a bucket number to each record in the IndexedValues table. All the records with indexes in the range from 0 to 1 are placed into 0th bucket, indexes in the range from 2 to 3 go into bucket number 1, etc. For each bucket find the maximum and minimum value.

```
select floor(index#/2) bucket, min(value), max(value)
from IndexedValues
group by floor(index#/2)
```

Logarithmic Buckets

A bird's-eye view onto big tables is essential for data analysis, with aggregation and grouping being the tools of the trade. Standard, equality-based grouping, however, fails to accommodate continuous distributions of data. Consider a *TaxReturns* table, for example. Would simple grouping by *GrossIncome* achieve anything? Undoubtedly it would show many individuals with identical incomes, but the big picture would escape us because of the sheer report size. Normally, we would like to know the distribution of incomes by ranges of values. Choosing the ranges carefully should produce a much more compact report.

There are two elementary methods for choosing ranges. With a linear scale the next range boundary point would be placed by a uniform offset. With a logarithmic scale the offset is increased exponentially. In the tax returns example a familiar linear scale of ranges is 0 – 10K, 10K – 20K, 20K – 30K, …, while the logarithmic scale is …, 1K –10K, 10K – 100K, 100K – 1000K, …

Although a linear scale is conceptually simpler, a logarithmic scale is more natural. It appears that a linear scale has more precision where most tax returns are located, but this is solely by virtue of the magic number 10K that was chosen as an increment. Had a different figure been chosen, say 100K, then the precision would have been lost.

In a capitalist system income is not bounded. There are numerous individuals whose income goes far beyond the ranges where most people exist. As of 2005 there were 222 billionaires in the US. They all do not fit in the same tiny 10K bucket of incomes, of course. Most likely each would be positioned in its unique range, so 222 10K ranges is necessary in order to accommodate only them!

From logarithmic perspective, however, a \$1B person is "only" 5 ranges away from a \$10K party. The logarithmic scale report is compact no matter how skewed the distribution is. Changing the factor of 10 into, say, 2 would increase the report size by a factor of $\log_2(10) \approx 3$, which could still qualify as a compact report. In a sense, the choice of factor in a logarithmic scale is irrelevant.

Logarithmic Scale in Programming

I often hear a fellow programmer suggesting "Let's allocate 2K of memory". Why 2K? Well, this size sounds about right for this particular data structure. Fine, if this structure is static, but what about dynamic ones, like any collection type? Allocating 2K every time when we need to grow the structure may be fine by today's standard, but this magic number 2K would look ridiculous a decade later.

Logarithmic scale, however, provides an immortal solution. "Last time I allocated X bytes of memory, let's allocate twice of that this time". In short, there is no room for linear solutions in the world abiding by Moore's law.

Let's implement logarithmic scale grouping of incomes in SQL. All that is needed is *power*, *log*, and *floor* functions:

```
select power(10,floor(log(10,GrossIncome))), count(1)
from TaxReturns
group by floor(log(10,GrossIncome));
```

It is the *floor(log(10,GrossIncome))* function that maps logarithmically spaced range boundaries into a distinct numbers. We group by this expression, although for the purpose of the readability of the result set, it is convenient to transform the column expression within the select list into conventional salary units by exponentiating it.

Skyline Query

Suppose you are shopping for a new car, and are specifically looking for a big car with decent gas mileage. Unfortunately, you are trying to satisfy the two conflicting goals. If querying the *Cars* relation in the database, then all models that are worse than others by both criteria can be ignored. The remaining set of cars is called the *Skyline*.

Figure 3.8 shows the Skyline of all cars in a sample set of three models. The vertical axis is seating capacity while the horizontal axis is the gas mileage. The vehicles are positioned in such a way that their locations match their respective profiles. The Hummer is taller than the Ferrari F1 racing car, which reflects the difference in their seating accommodations: 4 vs. 1. The Ferrari protrudes to the right of the Hummer, because it has superior gas mileage.

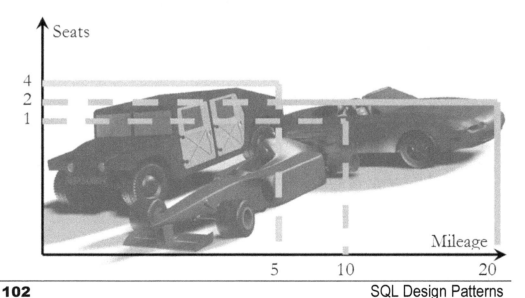

The Skyline is visualized as a contour of solid lines. The Ferrari outline is lost beneath the Roadster.

More formally the Skyline is defined as those points which are not dominated by any other point. A point dominates the other point if it is as good or better in all the dimensions. In the above example, the Roadster with *mileage=20* and *seating=2* dominates the Ferrari F1 with *mileage=10* and *seating=1*. This condition can certainly be expressed in SQL. In this example, the Skyline query is:

```
select * from Cars c
where not exists (
   select * from Cars cc
   where cc.seats >= c.seats and cc.mileage >  c.mileage
     or cc.seats >  c.seats and cc.mileage >= c.mileage
);
```

Despite the apparent simplicity of this query, you would not be pleased with this query performance. Even if the seats and mileage columns were indexed, it would not help much as only half of the records on average meet each individual inequality condition. Certainly, there are not many records that satisfy the combined predicate, but leveraging an index to match it is not possible. Bitmapped indexes, which excel with Boolean expressions similar to is here, demand a constant on one side of the inequality predicate.

There is an efficient way to answer a Skyline query[33]. Unfortunately, it is not aligned with the earlier Skyline SQL query attempt. Order all the data by either: seats, mileage, or mileage, seats. Here a composite index might be handy. Compare each record with its predecessor, and discard the one that is dominated by the other.

---

[33] We consider a two dimensional case only. An interested reader is referred to more elaborate methods in the paper by Stephan Börzsönyi, Donald Kossmann, Konrad Stocker: The Skyline Operator. http://www.dbis.ethz.ch/research/publications/38.pdf

Let's assume that this example has been extended to 4 records:

MANUFACTURER	SEATS	MILEAGE
Hummer	4	5
Ferrari	1	10
BMW	2	15
Roadster	2	20

Iterating record by record down, the Ferrari would be excluded first, because it is dominated by the neighbor BMW. Then, the BMW itself would be excluded, because it is dominated by the Roadster.

Relational Division

Relational Division is truly an exotic operator. Search any popular database forum for problems involving Relational Division. There certainly would be a few, but chances are they might be not recognized as such. For example, Chapter 1 problem 6 is almost a literal reproduction of the message posted at the newsgroup *microsoft.public.sqlserver.programming*. If nothing else, this section would help you to quickly identify a problem as Relational Division. After all, using the proper names is very important for effective communication.

Why it is called Division? It is the inverse of the (Cartesian) Product. Given a set of *JobApplicants*

Name
Steve
Pete
Kate

and a set of *JobRequirements,*

Language
SQL
Java

then the Cartesian Product *JobApplicants* ✕ *JobRequirements* is

Name	Language
Steve	SQL
Pete	Java
Kate	SQL
Steve	Java
Pete	SQL
Kate	Java

Inversely, given the *JobApplicants* ✕ *JobRequirements* relation (called the dividend), it could be divided by *JobRequirements* (the divisor) and *JobApplicants* (the quotient) would be obtained.

The analogy between relational algebra and arithmetic goes one step further. Relational division is similar to integer division. If the integer dividend x is not a multiple of integer divisor y, the quotient is defined as the maximal number q that satisfies the inequality:

$$x \geq q\,y$$

or the equality where r is called the *remainder*.

$$x = q\,y + r$$

In Relational Algebra, given a dividend X and divisor Y, the quotient Q is defined as a maximum relation that satisfies the inequality:

$$X \supseteq Q \times Y$$

or the equality:

$$X = Q \times Y \cup R$$

In the following example, the *JobApplicants* $\times$ *JobRequirements* relation is reduced to

Name	Language
Steve	SQL
Pete	Java
Kate	SQL
Kate	Java

which is appropriately called *ApplicantSkills*. Then,

ApplicantSkills = QualifiedApplicants $\times$ JobRequirements $\cup$ UnqualifiedSkills

where the quotient *QualifiedApplicants* is

Name
Kate

and the remainder *UnqualifiedSkills* is

Name	Language
Steve	SQL
Pete	Java

Informally, division identifies attribute values of the dividend that are associated with every member of the divisor, such as find job applicants who meet all job requirements.

Relational Division is not a fundamental operator. It can be expressed in terms of projection, Cartesian product, and set difference. The critical observation is that multiplying the projection[34] π_{Name}(ApplicantSkills) and *JobRequirements* results in the familiar Cartesian Product:

Name	Language
Steve	SQL
Pete	Java
Kate	SQL
Steve	Java
Pete	SQL
Kate	Java

Subtract *ApplicantSkills*, and project the result to get the *Name*s of all the applicants who are not qualified. Then, find all the applicants who are qualified as a complement to the set of all applicants. Formally:

```
QualifiedApplicants = πName(ApplicantSkills)-
- πName( πName(ApplicantSkills)×JobRequirements – ApplicantSkills )
```

Translating it into SQL is quite straightforward, although the resulting query gets quite unwieldy:

```
select distinct Name from ApplicantSkills
minus
select Name from (
    select Name, Language from (
        select Name from ApplicantSkills
    ), (
        select Language from JobRequirements
    )
    minus
    select Name, Language from ApplicantSkills
)
```

The minus operator is essentially an anti-join, so it is not surprising that it can be expressed in another form that is popular in the literature:

---

[34] This is the very first time I used the projection symbol. The Relational Algebra projection operator π_{Name}(ApplicantSkills) is the succinct equivalent to SQL query select distinct Name from ApplicantSkills

```
select distinct Name from ApplicantSkills i
where not exists (
    select * from JobRequirements ii
    where not exists (
        select * from ApplicantSkills iii
        where iii.Language = ii.Language
        and    iii.Name = i.Name
    )
)
```

Admittedly, this query is difficult to understand because of the double-negative construction – *not exists* clause inside another *not exists*. The reason for the double negation is SQL's inability to express universal quantification in the relational division query:

Name the applicants such that for all job requirements there exists a corresponding entry in the applicant skills

Mathematical logic is notorious for formal transformations of one logical expression into another. In this case

$$\forall x(\exists y\ f(x,y)\ )$$

is re-written into

$$\nexists x(\nexists y\ f(x,y)\ )$$

without too much thinking. The Relational division query becomes:

Name the applicants such that there is no job requirement such that there doesn't exists a corresponding entry in the applicant skills

which is a sloppy wording for the SQL query that was being analyzed.

As usual, the most elegant solution requires insight. The critical observation is expressing the informal Relational division query as:

Name the applicants for which the set of all job skills is a subset of their skills

It would be nice if SQL had a *subset* operator (also called *set containment*) so that we could write

```
select distinct Name from ApplicantSkills i
where (select Language from JobRequirements ii
        where ii.Name = i.Name)
    in (select Language from ApplicantSkills)
```

Here the SQL syntax has been abused and the already existing *in* operator leveraged to denote set containment. Without an explicit subset relation available it is expressed as the emptiness of the difference between the two sets. Formally,

$$A \subseteq B$$

is equivalent to

$$A \setminus B = \varnothing$$

Applied to our case it allows the transformation of the rough first attempt to a legitimate SQL query:

```
select distinct Name from ApplicantSkills i
where not exists (
    select Language from ApplicantSkills
    minus
    select Language from JobRequirements ii
    where ii.Name = i.Name
)
```

We are not done yet. Instead of checking the sets containment they could be simply counted instead!

```
select Name from ApplicantSkills s, JobRequirements r
where s.Language = r.Language
group by Name
having count(*) = (select count(*) from JobRequirements)
```

First, "irrelevant skills" were excluded by joining *ApplicantSkills* and *JobRequirements*. Now that the result is subset of the required skills, they are both counted and compared.

Relational division can have really bizarre applications. Consider finding the Greatest Common Divisor (GCD) for a set of integers.

Given a set of integers find the maximal integer that divides all of them.

The GCD problem is remarkable in a sense that it is connected to many areas of SQL programming. It is very tempting, for example, to define GCD as yet another user defined aggregate function. In this section, however, the GCD problem seems to be out of context, because the only thing that relates GCD and relational division is the word "division". It does not mean the same thing in both cases, however. Or does it?

It is the universal quantifier $\forall$ in our informal GCD query which makes the connection to the relational division. For illustration purposes we'll find the GCD of just three numbers 9, 15 and 42. Let's try making this query fit formally into the relational division framework. First it is a good idea to simplify a query in order to exclude the aggregation:

Given a set of integers, e.g. 9, 15, and 42 find another set of integers such that each of them divides all the numbers from the first set.

Admittedly, this query does not look like relational division at all. The relational division operator has two inputs: the dividend relation and the divisor relation. All there is so far is something that might measure up to the divisor role. Let's suppress the lingering doubt, and promote the relation formally to the divisor. In fact, why not even keep the *JobRequirements* relation name from the previous development?

Therefore, we have *JobRequirements*:

Language
9
15
42

What could be the missing *ApplicantSkills* dividend? The "Applicants" are really the integers; only those which have a "skill" to divide all the numbers listed in the *JobRequirements* would qualify. There we have *ApplicantSkills*!

Name	Language
2	2
2	4
2	6
...	...
3	3
3	6
3	9
...	...

This relation is imaginary, of course. The chapter on integer generators presented a way to generate all the integer pairs, and this method could in fact be adopted for this case. Next, simply plug in *JobRequirements* and *ApplicantSkills* into any of the relational division queries that were written in this chapter, say

```
select Name from ApplicantSkills s, JobRequirements r
where s.Language = r.Language
group by Name
having count(*) = (select count(*) from JobRequirements)
```

and we have the answer! There is one little optimization that can simplify the answer. The *ApplicantSkills.Language* column can be eliminated. Projection of the *ApplicantSkills* relation to the *Name* column is the familiar *Integers* relation. Now that there is no longer any column for the equijoin predicate *s.Language = r.Language*, the join condition between the *Integers* and *JobRequirements* demands the remainder of integer division to be *0*. With the names that were mindlessly borrowed from the sample relational division problem, the revised query may enter an obfuscated SQL coding contest.

```
select Name from (
    select num# as Name from Integers
    where num# <= (select min(language) from JobRequirements)
), JobRequirements
where mod(Language,Name)=0
group by Name
having count(*) = (select count(*) from JobRequirements)
```

With one more step, switching to more appropriate names, and we have the final GCD query:

```
select Divisor from (
    select num# as Divisor from Integers
    where num# <= (select min(Element) from NumberSet)
), NumberSet
where mod(Element, Divisor)=0
group by Divisor
having count(*) = (select count(*) from NumberSet)
```

The only remaining action is finding the maximum in the resulting set.

Outer Union

The union operator definition in Relational Algebra has a problem. It can be applied only to compatible relations that have identical attributes. The Outer Union operator, invented by E.F.Codd[35], can be applied to any pair of relations. Each relation is extended to the schema that contains all the attributes from both relations. The newly introduced columns are padded with NULLs. The resulting relations have the same schema and their tuples can, therefore, be combined together by an ordinary union.

Example. Suppose we have the *Personnel* relation

---

[35] Codd E.F. Extending the relational database model to capture more meaning. *ACM Transactions on Database Systems 4, 4(Dec), 1979.*

Dept	Emp
10	Smith
20	Jones

and the *Department*

Dept	Mgr
20	Blake
30	James

The outer union *Personnel* ∪ *Department* is

Dept	Emp	Mgr
10	Smith	null
20	Jones	null
20	null	Blake
30	null	James

This operator seems to have an extremely limited practical scope. The only usage of the outer union operator I'm aware of is the definition of (the full) outer join. Formally, the outer join of the relations A and B is defined in four steps:

1. Join both relations: $A \bowtie B$. In the example above we'll have

Dept	Emp	Mgr
20	Jones	Blake

2. Join both relations, project to the first relation schema and subtract the result from the first relation: $A \setminus \pi_{\text{sch}(A)} (A \bowtie B)$

Dept	Emp
10	Smith

3. Join both relations, project to the first relation schema and subtract the result from the first relation: $B \setminus \pi_{sch(B)} (A \bowtie B)$

Dept	Mgr
30	James

4. Apply outer union to the results of 1-3.

Dept	Emp	Mgr
10	Smith	null
20	Jones	Blake
30	null	James

This is actually the relational algebra versions of the outer union and outer join operations. Perhaps they should be properly named natural outer union and natural outer join. In SQL the two relations are always considered to have disjoint sets of attributes. In the following example, the outer union produces

Personnel.Dept	Department.Dept	Emp	Mgr
10	null	Smith	null
20	null	Jones	null
null	20	null	Blake
null	30	null	James

and outer join

Personnel.Dept	Department.Dept	Emp	Mgr
10	null	Smith	null
20	20	Jones	Blake
null	30	null	James

The formula connecting them is still valid, though.

Summary

- Extensible RDBMS supports user defined-aggregate functions. They could be either programmed as user-defined functions, or implemented by leveraging object-relational features.

- Rows could be transformed into columns via a pivot operator.

- Symmetric Difference is the canonic way to compare two tables.

- Logarithmic histograms provide a comprehensive summary of the data, which is immune to scaling.

- Relational division is used to express queries with the universal quantifier $\forall$ (i.e. "for all").

- Outer union can be applied to incompatible relations.

Exercises

Exercise 1:

Design a method to influence the order of summands of the LIST aggregate function.

Exercise 2:

Check the execution plan of the symmetric difference query in your database environment. Does it use set or join operations? If the former, persuade the optimizer to transform set into join. Which join method do you see in the plan? Can you influence the nested loops anti-join[36]? Is

---

[36] Nested Loops have acceptable performance with indexed access to the inner relation. The index role is somewhat similar to that of hash table in case of the Hash Join.

there noticeable difference in performance between all the alternative execution plans?

Exercise 3:

Binomial coefficient *x choose y* is defined by the formula where $n!$ is n-factorial.

$$\begin{bmatrix} x \\ y \end{bmatrix} = \frac{x!}{y!\,(x-y)!}$$

Implement it as SQL query.

Exercise 4:

Write down the following query informally in English.

```
select distinct Name from ApplicantSkills
```

Try to make it sound as close as possible to the Relational Division. What is the difference?

Exercise 5:

A tuple t_1 *subsumes* another tuple t_2, if t_2 has more NULL values than t_1, and they coincide in all non-NULL attributes. The minimum union of two relations is defined as an outer union with subsequent removal of all the tuples subsumed by the others. Suppose you have two relations R_1 and R_2 with all the tuples subsumed by the others removed as well. Prove that the outer join between R_1 and R_2 is the minimum union of R_1, R_2 and $R_1 \bowtie R_2$.

Exercise 6:

Check if your RDBMS of choice supplies some ad-hoc functions, which could be plugged into histogram queries. Oracle users are referred to *ntile* and *width_bucket*.

Exercise 7:

Write SQL queries that produce a natural outer union and a natural outer join.

Exercise 8:

Relational division is the prototypical example of a *set join*. Set joins relate database elements on the basis of sets of values, rather than single values as in a standard natural join. Thus, the division $R(x, y)/S(y)$ returns a set of single value tuples:

$$\{ (x) \mid \{y \mid R(x, y)\} \supseteq \{y \mid S(y)\} \}$$

More generally, one has the set-containment join of $R(x, y)$ and $S(y, z)$, which returns a set of pairs:

$$\{ (x, z) \mid \{y \mid R(x, y)\} \supseteq \{y \mid S(y, z)\} \}$$

In the job applicant's example the *JobRequirements* table can be extended with the column *JobName*. Then, listing all the applicants together with jobs they are qualified for is a set containment query; write it in SQL.

SQL Constraints

CHAPTER

Introduction

Constraints are fundamental to databases and application programming. Unfortunately, in the programming industry the discussion about constrains often degrades to a rather shallow dilemma. Should the constraints be enforced in the database, or in the application/middle tier?

If the reader is still undecided about this[37], then it makes little sense to continue. Constraint implementation in the database matured to a fairly sophisticated level, not the least of which should be credited to the wealth of the underlying language – SQL.

As the reader is assumed to be familiar with the basics of database constraints – unique key, referential integrity, check constraint, this chapter will venture into an obscure area of complex constraints. SQL standard allows declaring complex constraints as ASSERTIONs, but no database vendor supports them. For quite some time database triggers were the only complex constraint enforcement technique. This chapter will help the reader to broaden that view.

---

[37] As Marshall Spight put it: "I will not forgive you ☺ if you don't at least mention a few of the worst problems with application-enforced constraints:

1) not declarative

2) not centrally enforced—may be bypassed

3) application-language specific!"

Certain constraints can be implemented with the *Function Based* method. It might not be as general as the materialized views based technique, but it certainly is not short of elegance. The materialized views based method, on the other hand, is somewhat elaborate, although much more powerful. It is the favorite in this chapter.

Function Based Constraints

Function based constraints require little introduction. Sooner or later every database person comes across a unique constraint on UPPER(person.name). The other popular example of a function based constraint is:

```
alter table Emp
ADD CONSTRAINT namesInUppercase CHECK ( UPPER(ename)=ename )
```

This chapter will show the many reasons why declarative constraints declaration is always better than any alternative solution. I witnessed that in my own experience. Consider the query:

```
select * from emp
where ename like 'MIL%'
```

When I saw the following query execution plan, I was puzzled where did the second conjunct UPPER(ename) like UPPER('MIL%') come from?

OPERATION	OBJECT NAME
⊟ SELECT STATEMENT	
⊟ TABLE ACCESS	EMP
⊟ O🌿Filter Predicates	
⊟ ∧ AND	
⊟ ENAME LIKE 'MIL%'	
⊟ UPPER(ENAME) LIKE 'MIL%'	

The plan looked as if the optimizer rewrote the query into:

```
select * from emp
where ename like 'MIL%'
and UPPER(ename) like 'MIL%'
```

The answer may be immediate here in hindsight of the constraint that I declared earlier, but in practice I totally forgot about the constraint which I declared a while ago. After quick investigation, I indeed found that there was a check constraint *UPPER(ename) = ename* declared upon the *Emp* table. In other words, the RDBMS engine leverages constraints when manipulating query predicates.

What is the point of adding one more filter condition to a query that would execute correctly anyway? Imagine that a function-based index was added upon an *UPPER(ename)* pseudo column. It might be used, even though the original query does not refer to any function within the predicate:

```
select * from emp
where ename like 'MIL%'
```

A query execution leveraging an index often means difference between life and death from a performance perspective.

The next section will experiment with a somewhat more elaborated function based constraint.

Symmetric Functions

Consider an inventory database of boxes:

```
table Boxes (
    length integer,
    width  integer,
    height integer
)
```

Box dimensions in the real world are generally not given in any specific order. The choice of which dimensions becomes length, width, and height is essentially arbitrary. However, what if we want to identify the boxes according to their dimensions? For example, the box with length=1, width=2, and height=3 is the same box as the one with length=3, width=1, and height=2. Furthermore, how about declaring a *unique dimensional* constraint? More specifically, any two boxes that have the same dimensions would not be allowed.

An analytical mind would have no trouble recognizing that the heart of the problem is the column ordering. The values of the length, width, and height columns can be interchanged to form another legitimate record! Therefore, why not introduce three pseudo columns, say A, B, and C such that:

$$A \leq B \leq C$$

Then, a unique constraint on A, B, C should satisfy the requirement! It could be implemented as a function based unique index, as long as A, B, C can be expressed analytically in terms of *length, width, height*. Piece of cake: C is the *greatest* of *length, width, height*; A is the *least* of them, but how is *B expressed?* Well, the answer is easy to write although difficult to explain:

```
B = least (greatest (length,width),
greatest (width,height),
greatest (height,length) )
```

A mathematical perspective, as usual, clarifies a lot. Consider the following cubic equation:

$$x^3 + a\,x^2 + b\,x + c = 0$$

If roots x_1, x_2, x_3 are known, then the cubic polynomial could be factored as the following:

$$(x - x_1)\,(x - x_2)\,(x - x_3) = 0$$

Marrying both equations, coefficients *a*, *b*, *c* are expressed in terms of roots x_1, x_2, x_3:

$$a = -x_1 - x_2 - x_3$$

$$b = x_1\,x_2 + x_2\,x_3 + x_3\,x_1$$

$$c = -x_1\,x_2\,x_3$$

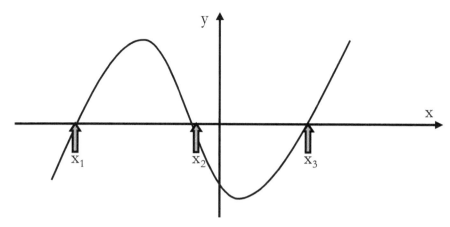

Figure 4.1 - *A shape of the graph of the polynomial $y=(x-x_1)(x-x_2)(x-x_3)$ is entirely defined by the roots x_1, x_2, and x_3. Exchanging them doesn't affect anything.*

The functions $-x_1-x_2-x_3$, $x_1x_2+x_2x_3+x_3x_1$, $-x_1x_2x_3$ are symmetric. Permuting x_1, x_2, x_3 has no effect on the values a, b, c. In other words, the order among the roots of cubic equation is irrelevant: formally, we speak of a set of roots, not a list of roots[38]. This is exactly the effect desired in the example with boxes. Symmetric functions rewritten in terms of length, width, height are:

```
length+width+height
length*width+width*height+height*length
length*width*height
```

Those expressions were simplified a little by leveraging the fact that the negation of a symmetric function is also symmetric.

The last solution is strikingly similar to the earlier one, where the greatest operator plays the role of multiplication, while the least operator goes as addition. It is even possible to suggest a solution, which is a mix-in between the two:

---

[38] Moreover, the roots are generally complex, so that the order is meaningless.

```
least(length,width,height)
least(length+width,width+height,height+length)
length+width+height
```

A reader can check that these three functions are again symmetric[39].

The last step is recording the solution in formal SQL:

```
table Boxes (
    length integer,
    width  integer,
    height integer
);

create unique index b_idx on Boxes(
    length + width + height,
    length * width + width * height + height * length,
    length * width * height
);
```

Symmetric functions provide a basis for a nifty solution. In practice however, a problem can often be solved by schema redesign. In the box inventory database example, a schema redesign is not necessary; simply change the practice of inserting unconstrained records *(length,width,height)* and demand that:

```
length ≥ width ≥ height
```

---

[39] Mathematically inclined readers are referred to the field of *Tropical* arithmetic, where the *least* operator plays the role of ordinary addition, and addition is taken the role of ordinary multiplication. This is how we've got the last set of symmetric functions – by just rewriting symmetric polynomials in tropical arithmetic.

Materialized View Constraints

Base relations – tables – and derived ones – views – are all fundamental building blocks of Relational databases. A derived relation may be virtual, meaning the defining relational expression is evaluated in terms of the base relations; or materialized, meaning the relation is actually stored. In database practice they are commonly referred to as plain views and materialized views, correspondingly.

In many respects a materialized view is similar to a base table. One can index it, declare a constraint, even (heaven forbid) associate a trigger. Declaring constraints upon materialized views turns out to be a very powerful method of enforcing complex constraints with limited SQL support.

In the database, research literature leveraging materialized views for constraint enforcement has been suggested as early as in 1978-1979[40]. Given that it was a long time before materialized views became a reality in practical RDBMS implementations, those ideas had to remain dormant. It was Tony Andrews who sparked a renewed interest in materialized view constraint enforcement in the Oracle community.

When declaring a constraint, the starting point is expressing it as a formal expression. Lets start analyzing how to represent the foreign key integrity constraint via materialized views. Please note carefully that we do this not because contemporary RDBMS engines lack foreign key support, or their implementation is deficient in any way. We do it solely because foreign key constraint is conceptually simple and yet

---

[40] Michael Hammer, Sunil Sarin. *Efficient Monitoring of Database Assertions.* ACM SIGMOD International Conference on Management of Data, 1978.

Peter Buneman, Eric Clemons. *Efficiently Monitoring Relational Databases.* ACM Transactions on Database Systems, Vol. 4, No. 3, Sept 1979, pages 368-382

semantically rich example which will provide a basis to further advance our technique. So, in plain English:

For any record in the Emp table there has to be a matching Dept record.

This constraint declaration is informal because of the term *matching*.

A more precise statement would read:

For any record e in the Emp table there has to exist a Dept d such that e.deptno = d.deptno.

It is generally a good idea to rephrase a constraint as an impossible condition. This does not really change anything from a logical perspective, but in real life, law enforcement implies some real world action, which has to be invoked whenever the law is broken. For example:

There doesn't exist a record e in the Emp table such that there is no Dept d such that e.deptno = d.deptno.

Admittedly, this sentence sounds awful (even for me, who wrote it in the first place). I can imagine how a reader without background in logic might feel. What is the point of elaborating formal content if at the end all that is produced is such gibberish as the last statement?

Well, this situation is common in math. An expression is transformed through a series of steps, so the expression might become ugly in the process, but sometimes luck gets involved and it finally collapses into a simple formula. In this example, it takes one more step

Consider all the record e in the Emp table such that there is no Dept d with e.deptno = d.deptno. There mustn't to be any!

before the statement finally contracts to:

The difference between the set of the Emp.dept and Dept.dept is empty.

It is formal, because it can be expressed in SQL, where the only missing part is equality between views:

```
select deptno from Emp
minus
select deptno from Dept
= ∅⁴¹
```

Let's refer to the view on the left side as *EmpWithoutDept*.

On afterthought, this assertion is obvious. The *Emp-Dept* referential integrity constraint is violated only if the *EmpWithoutDept* view becomes nonempty. It could happen when a tuple is inserted into the *Emp* table, or deleted from the *Dept* table.

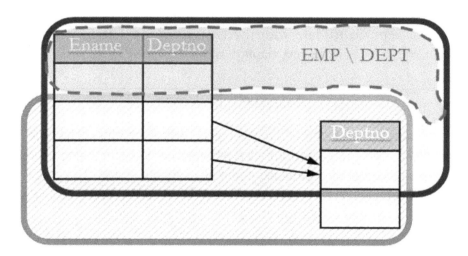

Figure 4.2 - *The record (Ename=SMITH, Deptno=10) doesn't match to any record in the department table: it belongs to the set* EMP \ DEPT. *The foreign key constraint asserts* EMP \ DEPT = ∅ .

---

⁴¹ If the reader is uncomfortable with the empty set symbol ∅, you can think of it as shorthand for

```
select deptno from dept where 1=0
```

Since there is no concept of equality between views in SQL, the condition for emptiness must be expressed by other means. If the *EmpWithoutDept* view is not empty, then *EmpWithoutDept.dept* is not NULL! A simple check constraint would do:

```
CREATE MATERIALIZED VIEW EmpWithoutDept AS
select deptno from Emp
minus
select deptno from Dept;

ALTER TABLE emp_minus_dept_mv
ADD CONSTRAINT EWD_is_empty CHECK( deptno is null );
```

Whenever a referential integrity constraint is violated, the *EmpWithoutDept* view becomes nonempty triggering a violation of the *EWD_is_empty* constraint.

While plain views do not require any maintenance, materialized views need to be kept up to date with the base relations. Efficient update of materialized views is achieved via *incremental evaluation*[42].

Incremental Evaluation

Queries and updates often do not get along with each other. They are conflicting goals from a performance perspective. We can speed up some queries at the cost of introducing some auxiliary structures. The most familiar examples of such structures are indexes and materialized views, and there are other cases which warrant a general concept.

Those structures need to be kept up to date with the base tables. Completely reevaluating them is out of question for any sizeable database. They have to be maintained incrementally: a change to the structure is small when the update transaction is small, which makes the overall

---

[42] Again, terminology used by database vendors varies. Oracle, for example, calls incrementally updateable materialized views *fast refreshable*.

performance acceptable. Incremental query evaluation is one of the most important performance ideas in the database world.

In practice we have to deal with database implementations which dictate seemingly arbitrary limitations on what operations do support incremental refresh and which ones do not. Oracle circa 2005 does not support set operators in the definition of incrementally maintained materialized views, for example. There is a workaround this limitation, though. The assertion could be rewritten into an equivalent form that leverages only supported operators:

```
CREATE MATERIALIZED VIEW EmpOuterJoinDept
REFRESH FAST ON COMMIT AS
select d.deptno ddept, d.rowid drid, e.rowid erid
from Emp e, Dept d
where e.deptno=d.deptno(+);

ALTER TABLE EmpOuterJoinDept
ADD CONSTRAINT ck_oj_mv CHECK(ddept is not null);
```

However, one especially attractive feature is lost: this materialized view is no longer empty.

Trigger Solution is Unreliable

A comparison between the materialized view and trigger based solution does not favor the latter. First, the trigger has to cover all operations: insert, update and delete – missing any of them would allow integrity violation. Second, a constraint involving more than one table has to be covered by multiple triggers as in the example on both *Emp* and *Dept* tables.

More important, however, is that writing triggers is a challenging exercise from concurrency semantics perspective. It is better to delegate complex code to RDBMS engine developers, and leverage the high level features that RDBMS offers.

In general, constructing incrementally updateable materialized views with such limitations becomes a coding exercise that tests one's patience. It is almost always possible to express an operator in a chain of incrementally refreshable materialized views. Here is how the minus operator can be represented:

```
create materialized view empDepts as
select deptno, count(*) cnt
from emp
group by deptno;

create materialized view deptEmpCross as
select dept.deptno dd, empDepts.deptno ed, dept.rowid drid, empDepts.rowid
erid
from empDepts, dept;

create materialized view deptEmpJoin as
select dept.deptno dd, empDepts.deptno ed, dept.rowid drid, empDepts.rowid
erid
from empDepts, dept
where dept.deptno=empDepts.deptno;

create materialized view deptEmpUnion as
select '1' marker,dd,rowid rid
from deptEmpCross
union all
select '2' marker,dd,rowid rid
from deptEmpJoin;

create materialized view deptCounts as
select dd, count(*) c
from deptEmpUnion
group by dd;

create materialized view empDeptCount as
select count(*) c
from empDepts;

create materialized view Final as
select dd, c1.rowid rid1, c2.rowid rid2
from empDeptCount c1, deptCounts c2
where c1.c=c2.c;
```

The basic idea is that a set difference can be expressed via joins and aggregation with counting, and an incremental refresh of the latter operations is supported. This is pointless from a practical perspective, however. It is hard to imagine that anybody would buy the overhead of 7 (!) nonempty materialized views for a mere set difference implementation.

Sooner or later incremental refresh limitations will be lifted. For the purpose of further constraint study in this book, let's continue pretending as if it already happened.

Disjoint Sets

Enforcing that the two tables have no common records is a very common practical problem. Consider a typical Object-Oriented design scenario where the *Employee* type has two subtypes: *FullTimeEmp* and *PartTimeEmp*. On the database side, suppose that there are only two tables: *FullTimeEmp* and *PartTimeEmp*. What should be done to enforce the uniqueness of an employee *id*? Certainly, both *FullTimeEmp.id* and *PartTimeEmp.id* can be declared to be unique, but how do we guarantee that there is no employee, who is both full time and part time? These sets have to be disjointed:

```
CREATE MATERIALIZED VIEW fullTime_intersect_partTime
select id from FullTimeEmp
intersect
select id from PartTimeEmp

ALTER TABLE fullTime_intersect_partTime
ADD CONSTRAINT disjointClasses CHECK(id is null)
```

There is another, more straightforward, but somewhat cumbersome way to approach this problem. Like any other constraint, a unique key can be enforced via a materialized view as well. Let's start with the smaller and easier task of defining *FullTimeEmp.id* unique key. Suppose that *FullTimeEmp* has two more columns: *name* and *startedAt*. Again, we begin rephrasing the constraint as an impossible condition:

The two employee records e_1 and e_2 are contradictory whenever $e_1.id = e_2.id$, and yet either $e_1.name \neq e_2.name$ or $e_1.startedAt \neq e_2.startedAt$. No contradictory employee records are allowed.

It easy to express this constraint formally:

```
CREATE MATERIALIZED VIEW contradictoryEmployees
select e1.id id from FullTimeEmp e1, FullTimeEmp e2
where e1.id = e2.id and (
      e1.name <> e2.name or e1.startedAt <> e2.startedAt
)

ALTER TABLE fullTime_intersect_partTime
ADD CONSTRAINT disjointClasses CHECK(id is null)
```

It is obvious that the number of inequality comparisons would grow with the number of columns in the table. This is why I referred to this approach as cumbersome. Some RDBMS implementations introduce a *ROWID* pseudo column, which is guaranteed to be unique. This allows comparing *ROWID*s instead of actual values:

```
CREATE MATERIALIZED VIEW contradictoryEmployees
select e1.id id from FullTimeEmp e1, FullTimeEmp e2
where e1.id = e2.id and e1.rowid <> e2.rowid

ALTER TABLE fullTime_intersect_partTime
ADD CONSTRAINT disjointClasses CHECK(id is null)
```

Without *ROWID*s the constraint is actually weaker than a unique key, as it cannot distinguish duplicate records. Duplicate records do not exist in set semantics, but SQL operates with bags. One extra nested materialized view is needed to exclude duplicates.

The final solution is only one step away. Simply declare the unique key constraint on a materialized view, which is the union of *FullTimeEmp* and *PartTimeEmp* tables. However, the *union* is not defined on tables which are *incompatible,* and in fact, it is easy to imagine that tables corresponding to different subclasses have different attributes. The concern about union not being defined for incompatible relations has already been addressed in the previous chapter, where the outer union was introduced.

There is another reason why this solution is less elegant than the one with disjoint set constraint. The outer join view is not empty, which implies storage overhead. Although in principle the RDBMS engine could flatten nested materialized views, do not expect this to be implemented anytime soon.

Disjoint Intervals

Consider a list of intervals:

```
table Intervals (
    head integer,
    tail integer
)
```

We would like to declare these intervals as mutually disjoint.

In math, disjoint intervals are defined as sets that do not intersect with each other[43]. This definition, however, is not very useful in this situation since the intervals disjoint condition must be formulated in terms of intervals boundaries.

Once more the constraint is rephrased as an impossible condition:

The intervals [head₁,tail₁] and [head₂,tail₂] overlap whenever head₂ is between head₁ and tail₁. No overlapping intervals are allowed.

Wait a minute, something must be wrong here! The interval overlapping condition has to be symmetric with respect to both intervals, but the formal statement written does not look symmetric at all. Indeed, what if interval *[head2,tail2]* covers *[head1,tail1]*? Then *head2* is not between *head1* and *tail1*, and yet the intervals do overlap. This non-symmetry is illusory, however.

---

[43] More precisely, intervals $[head_1, tail_1]$ and $[head_2, tail_2]$ intersect whenever there is a point x such that x $\in [head_1, tail_1]$ and x $\in [head_2, tail_2]$.

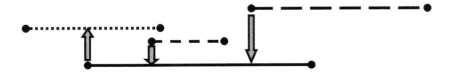

Figure 4.3 - *Overlapping intervals always have the head of one interval bounded between the ends of the other interval.*

Let's write the constraint formally:

```
CREATE MATERIALIZED VIEW overlapping_intervals
select i1.head h
from intervals i1, intervals i2
where i2.head between i1.head and i1.tail

ALTER TABLE overlapping_intervals
ADD CONSTRAINT no_overlapping_intervals CHECK(h is null)
```

This query shows that *i1* and *i2* iterate over the set of all intervals, each pair of intervals *[a,b]* and *[c,d]* in the set would be considered twice: first time when *i1.head = a, i1.tail = b, i2.head = c, i2.tail = d*, and second time when *i1.head = c, i1.tail = d, i2.head = a, i2.tail = b*. This reasoning, however, exposes a bug in the implementation. Could *i1* and *i2* be the same interval? One more predicate must be added that excludes this possibility:

```
CREATE MATERIALIZED VIEW overlapping_intervals
select i1.head h
from intervals i1, intervals i2
where i2.head between i1.head and i1.tail
and (i2.head <> i1.head or i2.tail <> i1.tail)

ALTER TABLE overlapping_intervals
ADD CONSTRAINT no_overlapping_intervals CHECK(h is null)
```

Alternatively, an asymmetric join condition could have been used, and each pair of intervals only considered once. A ***total*** order is defined among all the intervals so that for each pair of intervals *i1* and *i2* either *i1* **precedes** *i2*, or *i2* precedes *i1*. The lexicographical order comparison predicate *i2.head < i1.head or (i2.head = i1.head and i2.tail < i1.tail)* defines a total order. The constraint can now be written as follows:

Consider all the pairs of intervals such that [head₁,tail₁] precedes [head₂,tail₂]. They overlap whenever head₂ is less than or equal to tail₁. Again, no overlapping intervals are allowed.

And formally as:

```
CREATE MATERIALIZED VIEW overlapping_intervals
select i1.head h
from intervals i1, intervals i2
where (i2.head < i1.head or
       i2.head = i1.head and i2.tail < i1.tail)
  and i2.head <= i1.tail

ALTER TABLE overlapping_intervals
ADD CONSTRAINT no_overlapping_intervals CHECK(h is null)
```

Temporal Foreign Key Constraint

An audit trail is a database design in which records are never deleted. All data modifications are logged into temporal tables. Every record in a temporal table obtains two timestamp attributes: *CREATED* and *DELETED*. The values of the other attributes are valid during the interval starting with *CREATED* date and ending with *DELETED* date. Now that the same record of values is scattered into many records, how are constraints enforced? Specifically, given two tables with parent-child relationship, how is referential constraint between their "temporalized" versions also enforced?

```
table HistParent (
   id integer,
   ...,
   created date,
   deleted date);

table HistChild (
   pid integer,    -- foreign key to HistParent.id???
   ...,
   created date,
   deleted date
);
```

The constraint is formulated, first informally in English, then in SQL. A child record can be created only if its parent record already exists. Likewise, a parent record cannot be deleted until it has at least one child. Informally,

A child lifespan must be contained within the parent lifetime.

The critical issue is defining the parent and child lifetimes.

Since each parent is identified by the *id* attribute, it is quite easy to define its lifetime. The lifetime of a parent is the longest span of time covered by the chain of *[created, deleted]* intervals. Now the interval coalesce technique from Chapter 1 can be invoked, and the parent lifetime view obtained:

```
view ParentLifetime (
   id integer,
   birth date,
   death date
);
```

Please note that all the attributes marked by ellipsis in the *HistParent* table are gone. In a way the interval coalesce operation is similar to aggregation, but unlike aggregation, coalesce produces more than one aggregate value.

If a set of attributes identifying the child is present, then its lifetime could simply be defined the same way the parent's lifetime is defined. We don't have to, though! Instead of gluing the smaller *[created, deleted]* child intervals into the larger *[birth, death]*, we just observe that if each individual *[created, deleted]* interval is contained in the parent lifetime, so also is the child lifetime.

Now everything is ready for formal constraint expression. The following query enumerates all the child records that violate the temporal referential integrity constraint. Therefore, it should be empty:

```
select * from HistChild c where not exists
   (select * from ParentLifetime p
    where p.id = c.pid
    and c.created between p.birth and p.death
    and c.deleted between p.birth and p.death
   )
```

Cardinality Constraint

The materialized view constraint enforcement method is like a hammer looking for a nail to strike. Cardinality constraints, that is, ensuring that a table has certain number of rows, surely fall into the nail category. Sometimes, there is a more ingenious solution.

Consider a table with 3 columns A, B, C, and functional dependency $\varnothing \to \{A,B,C\}$. In general, the functional dependency $X \to Y$ requires each pair of rows that agree on the columns from the set X to agree on the columns from Y, as well. In other words, there is no couple of rows such that they agree on column set X and disagree on Y. In the case of functional dependency $\varnothing \to \{A,B,C\}$ this means no two rows unconditionally disagree on values of the columns A, B, C. These are the only columns in the table; therefore, all rows are identical! If duplicates are disallowed by enforcing unique key constraint, then a constraint is effectively enforced limiting table cardinality to 1, at most.

SQL lacks the ability to declare and enforce functional dependency constraints. A unique key is special case of functional dependency constraint $X \to Y$, where Y contains all table columns. Unfortunately, unique keys with the empty set of columns are not allowed in SQL.

In one of the soap boxes in Chapter 1 we had discussed a similar problem with *group by* operator that did not admit empty sets either. As a workaround, a calculated pseudo column was introduced. Let's amend the table with extra column[44]:

---

[44] The solution is credited to Jarl Hermansson

```
table T (
   A integer,
   B integer,
   C integer,
   dummyCol integer default 0 not null check (dummyCol = 0) unique
)
```

The combination of the check constraint and the uniqueness constraint guarantees that no more than one row is allowed. Elegant solutions always trigger the same reaction: "Why didn't I think of that?"

Summary

- Materialized views provide the most comprehensive way to implement complex constraints.

- Constraints of any kind which are declared within RDBMS are superior to any alternative procedural solution. Your query can be rewritten by optimizer to leverage constraint expression predicates.

- Be careful with concurrency issues when implementing constraints via triggers (or any other procedural way for that matter).

Exercises

Exercise 1:

Provide a set of symmetric functions of four variables.

Exercise 2:

What other operations besides +, *, *least*, and *greatest* can you suggest? What laws must these operations meet?

Exercise 3:

Write down the *ParentLifetime* view definition.

Exercise 4:

Implement the *unique(n)* constraint, which permits no more than *n* rows to have any given value.

Exercise 5:

Implement a functional dependency constraint that restricts each *Emp.job* to a certain *Emp.sal* range. In other words, no two employees can have the same job, and have their salaries in different ranges. Use the expression *floor(log(10,Emp.sal))* from Chapter 3 that maps salaries into logarithmic buckets.

Trees in SQL

Introduction

Graphs and trees are ubiquitous data structures. They do not easily fit into a Relational model; therefore querying them requires a little bit more ingenuity than the routine select-project-join.

Compared to graphs, trees are relatively simple creatures. They are easy to draw. Almost any problem involving a tree structure is easy to solve. Algorithms on trees are generally fast. Edges, which are very important in graph definition, can be almost completely ignored for a tree. The tree structure could be encrypted in the nodes alone, and those tree encodings could be invented almost on a daily basis.

Most of this chapter will focus on tree encodings. The rest is dedicated to smaller problems such as node ordering by ad-hoc criteria. Yet, several problems are postponed until the next chapter, wherein hierarchical aggregate queries and tree comparisons will be studied. A reader who is primarily looking to develop some intuition with vendor specific hierarchical SQL extensions (be that the *connect by*, or the recursive *with* operator) is advised to proceed to the next chapter.

Materialized Path

Tree is a subclass of graph. However, since graphs are more complex entities with their own set of problems, they will not be explored in depth in this chapter.

For all practical purposes a tree can be defined as a set of nodes arranged into a hierarchical structure via tree encoding. The purpose of tree encoding is to assign a special label to each node and to manipulate tree nodes – i.e. query and update – by means of those labels. Informally, each node is equipped with a global positioning device that transmits the node's coordinates. Once each node's geographical position is known, typical queries such as the following can be answered:

Count all the employees who are located south of the "King", in other words, who report directly or indirectly to him.

Without a doubt you are already familiar with at least one such encoding: a UNIX directory structure[45]. Each file location in the hierarchy is defined by an absolute pathname -- a chain of directories that a user has to navigate from root to the leaf of the hierarchy. For example, /usr/bin/ls is an absolute pathname. On the top of the directory structure there is a directory called *usr*, which contains a directory called *bin*, which contains a file called *ls*.

This seemingly straightforward idea can be applied to any tree structure. First, discover or cook up some unique key, which would distinguish the node's children. Then, list all the ancestor unique keys as the node's encoding. This list can be represented as a string (if so, there must be agreement upon a string delimiter), or as a collection datatype. This encoding will be referred to as *materialized path*. The adjective *materialized* emphasizes the fact that the path is stored. If the path is built dynamically, then the adjective is omitted and thus this dynamically generated encoding is referred to as simply *path*[46].

---

[45] Ignoring symbolic links

[46] The reader undoubtedly noticed the parallel to view/materialized view terminology.

Employee Name	Encoding
⊟ KING	1
⊟ JONES	1.1
⊟ SCOTT	1.1.1
⊟ ADAMS	1.1.1.1
⊟ FORD	1.1.2
⊟ SMITH	1.1.2.1
⊟ BLAKE	1.2
⊟ ALLEN	1.2.1
⊟ WARD	1.2.2
⊟ MARTIN	1.2.3

Table 5.1 - *Organization chart encoded with a materialized path. Each of the node's children is enumerated with integer numbers and a designated dot as a delimiter.*

At this moment, there is enough expressive power for basic queries:

An employee JONES and all his (indirect) subordinates:

```
select e1.ename from emp e1, emp e2
where e1.path like e2.path || '%'
and e2.ename = 'JONES'
```

An employee FORD and the chain of his supervisors:

```
select e1.ename from emp e1, emp e2
where e2.path like e1.path || '%'
and e2.ename = 'FORD'
```

Usually, query performance is unrelated to the form in which the query is written in SQL. In principle, a query optimizer has powerful techniques for transforming any query into an equivalent, better performing expression. Not in this case!

The first query is fine. The matching a string prefix is roughly equivalent to a range check where chr(255) is the last ASCII code:

```
select e1.ename from emp e1, emp e2
where e1.path between e2.path and e2.path || chr(255)
and e2.ename = 'JONES'
```

A reasonable execution strategy would be finding the unique employee record *e2* matching *ename='JONES'*, first. Finding a unique record is typically done via an index lookup, in other words, extremely fast. The first query execution step establishes the range of paths, which the *e1.path* encoding has to fall into. If this range of paths does not contain too many paths, then the best way to find them is to iterate via the index range scan. The more subordinates JONES has, the longer it will take to output them. In other words, the speed of this query is determined by the size of the output – there is hardly a more efficient way to express this query.

The equivalent range check rewriting is valid for the second query as well:

```
select e1.ename from emp e1, emp e2
where e2.path between e1.path and e1.path || chr(255)
and e2.ename = 'FORD'
```

Unlike the previous case, however, now not only is the interval of paths known, but also the path *e2.path* itself, which will be matched against all the intervals of the *e1* table. Certainly, there would not be that many paths that match with *e2.path*, because the chain of ancestors in a balanced hierarchy is never too long.

Yet, there is no obvious index that could leverage this idea. The condition of a point belonging to an interval consists of the two predicates *e2.path* $>=$ *e1.path* and *e2.path* $<=$ *e1.path* $||$ *chr(255)*. A normal B-Tree index on the *e1.path* column could be leveraged while processing the first predicate only, and it would have to scan half of the records on average[47].

---

[47] There are specialized indexing schemes – R-Tree, Interval tree, etc – that approach this problem. It remains to be seen if they could ever enjoy the same level of adoption as B-Tree and bitmapped indexes.

Finding a Set of Intervals Covering a Point

Querying ranges is asymmetric from a performance perspective. It is easy to answer if a point falls inside some interval, but it is hard to index a set of intervals that contain a given point. Applied to nested sets, there will be difficulty in answering queries about the node's ancestors.

The critical observation is that a chain of ancestors is encoded in the node's materialized path encoding. The database does not have to be accessed in order to tell that the ancestors of nodes 1.5.3.2 are nodes 1.5.3, 1.5, and 1. A simple function could parse the materialized path. This function's "natural habitat" is the client side. There a dynamic SQL query is built:

```
select ename from emp
where path in ('1.5.3', '1.5', '1')
```

On the server side the implementation could be little bit more sophisticated. The list of ancestors can be implemented as a temporary table built by a table function. This sketchy idea will be developed in greater detail in later sections where more elegant encodings than the materialized path will be studied.

This section concludes with a materialized path tree encoding schema design:

```
table TreeNodes (
    path varchar2(2000),   ...
)
```

This schema leaves the structure of the *TreeNodes.path* column unspecified. Ideally, some constraints could be added, but once again, a much nicer development that does not require string parsing techniques awaits us ahead.

Nested Sets

Another approach to a tree structure is modeling it as nested sets.

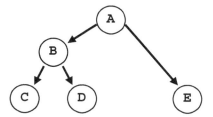

Figure 5.2a - *A tree.*

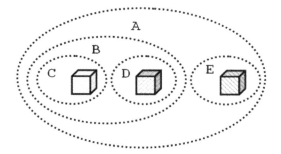

Figure 5.2b - *Nested sets structure for the tree at fig. 5.2a. Set elements are boxes, and sets are the ovals including them. Every parent set contains its children sets.*

Set containment could clearly accommodate any tree. To grow a tree by adding a new child, one more set is simply nested into the appropriate parent set.

Naive nested sets implementation would materialize a set of elements at each node. Aside from the fact that the RDBMS of your choice has to be capable operating with sets at the datatype level[48], this implementation would be quite inefficient. Every time a node is inserted into a tree, the chain of all the containing sets should be expanded to include at least one more element.

A more sophisticated variant of Nested Sets has been widely popularized by Joe Celko. The main idea behind this encoding is representing nested sets as intervals of integers as shown in Figure 5.3.

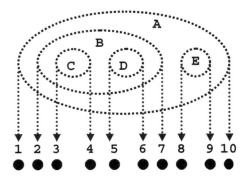

Figure 5.3 - *Nested Sets as intervals of integers. Node B is encoded by the interval beginning with 2 and ending with 7.*

Unlike the first naïve nested sets implementation, where there must be a set datatype in order to be able to check if one set encoding contains another encoding, Celko's encoding no longer needs it.

The schema for nested sets tree encoding:

```
table EmpHierarchy (
    left integer,
    right integer,
    ename varchar(2000),
    ...
)
```

---

[48] High-end databases indeed have support for collection datatypes.

SQL Design Patterns

A typical query checks if one interval is covered by the other interval, which can be easily expressed via a standard SQL. For example the following query finds the chain of *SMITH*'s supervisors:

```
select node1.ename
from EmpHierarchy node1, EmpHierarchy node2
where node1.left between node2.left and node2.right
and node2.ename = 'SMITH'
```

This query is essentially the same as querying the chain of ancestors in the section on materialized path encoding. It raises the concern about this query's performance. The dynamic SQL trick, which was employed for materialized path encoding, however, no longer works. There is no way to know the position of the node in the hierarchy by looking at the encoding of that node alone.

Like the naïve nested sets, intervals of integers encoding is volatile. Unlike naïve nested sets, inserting a new node involves a lot more work – roughly half of the nodes must be recomputed.

The crux of the problem is that integers are not dense. There is always a limit onto the number of intervals that can be nested inside any given interval of integers.

Fortunately, integers have nothing to do with interval nesting. They excel for illustration purposes, but if non-volatile encoding is the goal, dense domains of numbers, like rational or real numbers are used. With this objective in mind, how intervals of rational numbers are nested will be shown. The first step though is to learn how to divide an interval into smaller pieces.

Interval Halving

Consider splitting an interval with rational endpoints into two smaller intervals. Any point between the left and the right endpoint might be good enough to the extent that there are two intervals. On the other hand, if this point is chosen carelessly, then one interval might be much smaller than the other one. This might be a problem from an implementation perspective, because small intervals impose stricter requirements on the arithmetic's precision.

For example, checking if point 0.7453 belongs to the interval [0.3, 0.9] is much easier than if it belongs to the interval [0.743, 0.748] since there is no need to go no further than one digit comparison in the first case versus three digits in the second. Therefore, the "most economical" way of finding the point between the two must be sought after.

For repetition sake, given two rational numbers, what is the simplest number between them? Most people would probably choose the arithmetic average. For example, the simplest number between 0 and ½ is ¼, the simplest number between ¼ and ½ is 3/8 and so on. If we start with the point 0 and 1 and continue on halving the intervals iteratively then, what kind of numbers would be produced? Clearly, those whose denominator is a power of 2, or simply, dyadic fractions.

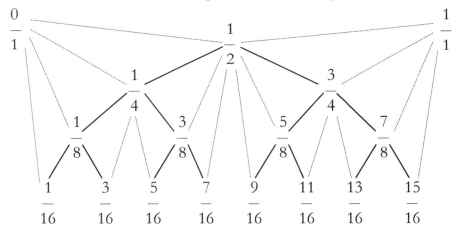

Figure 5.4 - *Halving interval [0,1] produces dyadic fractions that are naturally organized into a binary tree.*

Elementary school students might beg to differ. When questioned what the sum of ½ and ¼ is some suggest that the result is ½ + ¼ =

$(1+1)/(2+4) = 2/6 = 1/3$[49]. Ironically, their naïve approach is not without merit. The operation of adding fractions in this "wrong way" is called the mediant. The mediant is the simplest number between two fractions if using the smallness of a denominator as a measure of simplicity. Indeed, the average of ¼ and ½ has denominator 8, while the mediant has denominator 3.

If we start with the point 0 and 1 and continue on taking the mediant iteratively; then another famous set of numbers, Farey fractions, is produced.

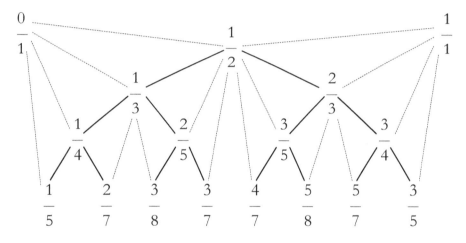

Figure 5.5 - *Dividing interval [0,1] by taking a mediant produces Farey fractions organized into Stern-Brocot tree.*

The two systems of rational numbers just described are very closely related. In fact, there is a fascinating map between them, but the details are perhaps too advanced for this SQL programming book. An interested reader might want to google *Minkovski question mark function* for more information.

---

[49] In American educational system adding rational numbers correctly is a skill developed somewhere between middle school and college.

Although it is possible to develop nested interval tree encodings with both approaches, in this book only Farey fractions will be studied. The main reason is the encoding size. For the tree of dyadic fractions denominators, multiply by 2 at each next level. For Stern-Brocot tree denominators grow slightly slower, approximately as powers of 1.618, where 1.618 is the golden ratio. In other words, Farey fractions are the most economical way to organize a system of nested intervals.

From Binary to N-ary Trees

The idea of interval splitting applies to binary trees. It could be easily extended to general *n-ary* trees by a well known one-to-one mapping of binary trees to *n-ary* trees. The *n-ary* tree is transformed into a binary tree as follows.

Each parent node connected to the first child stays connected that way in the binary tree. Each next child is detached from its parent and is reconnected to its older sibling. Therefore, the second sibling has the first sibling as a parent in the binary tree; the third is connected to the second, and so on. The resulting tree is obviously binary, since each node has exactly two connections:

- The left child as a former first child in the *n-ary* tree.

- The right child as a former younger sibling in the *n-ary* tree.

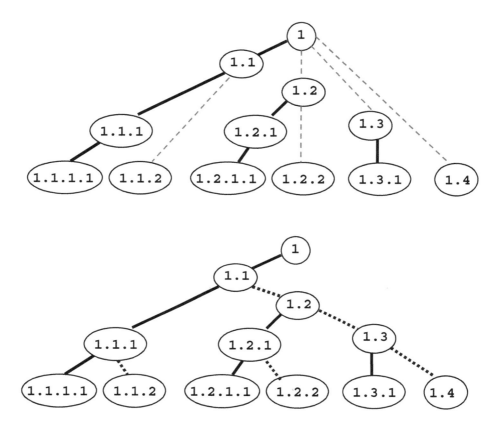

Figure 5.6 - *Mapping n-ary into binary tree could be viewed as a reorganization of edges between the tree nodes. A link between a parent and its first child remains unchanged, while a link from a younger child is transferred to the older sibling.*

Let's transform the binary tree in Figure 5.5 into an *n-ary* tree. The root node has one child only. Therefore, it is convenient to agree that the root node of the binary tree in Figure 5.5 is 1/1 rather than ½. Then, node ½ is the first child, 2/3 is the second child, and so on. The first child of ½ is 1/3, the second child is 2/5, etc as shown in Figure 5.7.

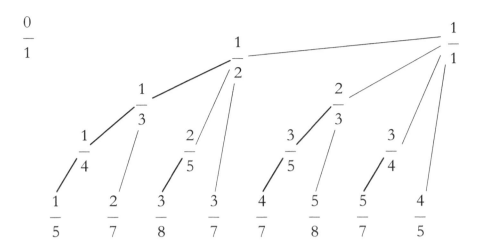

Figure 5.7 - *Stern-Brocot binary tree reorganized into n-ary tree.*

Let's wrap these vague ideas into more rigorous form. The next section will show that Farey fractions are essentially *continued fractions* which leads to a simple algebra problem of 2×2 matrices. Matrices are required because matrix multiplication mimics materialized paths concatenation. Our development is essentially translating the algebra of materialized path strings into a matrix form.

Matrix Encoding

The very basic skill of multiplying 2×2 matrices of integer numbers is listed as a reminder in Figure 5.8.

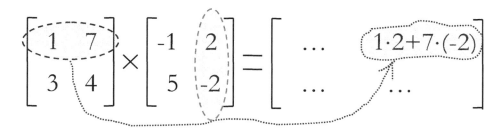

Figure 5.8 - *Multiplying 2×2 matrices. Each row in the left operand is matched element by element against a column in the right operand.*

Matrix multiplication obeys the same rules as string concatenation. It is associative

$$(AB)C = A(BC)$$

and distributive

$$AB + AC = A(B+C)$$

but not commutative

$$AB \neq BA$$

Any materialized path is a concatenation of *atomic* materialized paths. For example, .1.3.2.5 can be viewed as .1 linked to .3, then joined with .2, and finally connected to .5. Can the same thing be done with matrices? The trick is to define atomic matrices, such that multiplying them would produce the matrix encoding for the full path.

Atomic matrices turned out to be quite simple. In fact every atomic matrix has three constant entries: 0 in the lower right corner, and 1 in the lower left, and -1 in the upper right. The upper left entry is the node's sequence number in the chain of siblings incremented by 1. For example, .5 corresponds to the matrix:

$$\begin{bmatrix} 6 & -1 \\ 1 & 0 \end{bmatrix}$$

And the result from multiplying the matrices corresponding to *.1, .3, .2,* and *.5* is:

$$\begin{bmatrix} 2 & -1 \\ 1 & 0 \end{bmatrix} \cdot \begin{bmatrix} 4 & -1 \\ 1 & 0 \end{bmatrix} \cdot \begin{bmatrix} 3 & -1 \\ 1 & 0 \end{bmatrix} \cdot \begin{bmatrix} 6 & -1 \\ 1 & 0 \end{bmatrix} = \begin{bmatrix} 107 & -19 \\ 62 & -11 \end{bmatrix}$$

Although we didn't seem to progress much so far, we can at least round up matrix tree encoding schema design

```
table MatrixTreeNodes (
    a11 integer,
    a12 integer,
    a21 integer,
    a22 integer
);
```

A lot of questions might emerge in the reader's mind at this moment, and all of them will be addressed one by one. The most important of which is how this matrix encoding is related to nested intervals? Indeed, all these matrix manipulations should be evaluated from the querying perspective. In particular, how are the node's descendants and ancestors queried? And an even more basic question, how are the node's parent and immediate children found?

Parent and Children Queries

In the example

$$\begin{bmatrix} 2 & -1 \\ 1 & 0 \end{bmatrix} \cdot \begin{bmatrix} 4 & -1 \\ 1 & 0 \end{bmatrix} \cdot \begin{bmatrix} 3 & -1 \\ 1 & 0 \end{bmatrix} \cdot \begin{bmatrix} 6 & -1 \\ 1 & 0 \end{bmatrix} = \begin{bmatrix} 107 & -19 \\ 62 & -11 \end{bmatrix}$$

there are a certain constraints that node encoding obeys. The entries in the left column are positive, and the entries in the right column are negative. And absolute values of the entries in the right column are component-wise smaller than those in the left column. Likewise, absolute values in the upper row are greater than the absolute values in the lower row. These properties are obvious for atomic matrices, but what about arbitrary nodes?

Consider an arbitrary node with encoding as:

$$\begin{bmatrix} a_{11} & a_{12} \\ a_{21} & a_{22} \end{bmatrix}$$

Its n-th child encoding is calculated as a matrix product of:

$$\begin{bmatrix} a_{11} & a_{12} \\ a_{21} & a_{22} \end{bmatrix} \cdot \begin{bmatrix} n+1 & -1 \\ 1 & 0 \end{bmatrix} = \begin{bmatrix} a_{11}\,(n+1) + a_{12} & -a_{11} \\ a_{21}\,(n+1) + a_{22} & -a_{21} \end{bmatrix}$$

Let us examine this expression closely. First we notice that the parent left row entries are moved into the child right row with the sign changed. Now, can we prove our intuition about the entries in the left row being positive and the entries in the right row being negative? Sure. Assume this property holds in the case of the parent encoding. Then, it must carry over to the child. By induction, it follows that any node will honor it. A similar line of reasoning proves our insight about absolute values.

The second very important constraint that matrix encoding satisfies is:
$$a_{11}\,a_{22} - a_{12}\,a_{21} = 1$$

A reader with basic linear algebra background most likely recognized the matrix determinant there. Determinants obey multiplication law: when matrices multiply, their determinants multiply as well. Therefore, a determinant of the node encoding matrix is a product of the atomic matrix determinants! Since all atomic matrices have a determinant equal to 1, the determinant of any node encoding matrix must be 1.

A determinant constraint reduces the number of independent matrix entries to three. Given any three matrix elements, the forth entry is unambiguously calculated from the determinant constraint equation. And this could be done even better by reducing the number of independent elements to two.

Given the two elements $a11$ and $a21$, relabeled conventionally as a and $-b$, plus the unknowns: $a12$ and $a22$ relabeled as y and x, the determinant equation reads:

$$a\,x + b\,y = 1$$

This is perhaps the most celebrated equation in the elementary number theory. Its integer solutions are calculated via the extended Euclidean algorithm. Here is the algorithm illustrated on the familiar matrix encoding example:

$$\begin{bmatrix} 107 & -19 \\ 62 & -11 \end{bmatrix}$$

The following equation is solved in a series of steps illustrated in Figure 5.9:

$$107\, x - 62\, y = 1$$

```
107-1*62 =                                    = 1*107- 1*62  = 45
     ↙  ↓
62 -1*45 = 62          - 1*(1*107- 1*62)  = 2*62 - 1*107  = 17
     ↙  ↓
45 -1*17 = (1*107-1*62) - 2*(2*62 - 1*107) = 3*107 -5*62   = 11
     ↙  ↓
17 -1*11 = (2*62 -1*107) - 1*(3*107- 5*62) = 7*62 - 4*107  = 5
     ↙  ↓
11 -2*5  = (3*107-5*62) - 2*(7*62 - 4*107)
```

Figure 5.9 - *The extended Euclidean algorithm applied to numbers 107 and 62. We find an integer 1 such that 1*62 is no larger than 107, then show that the largest common measure of 62 and 107 is the same as largest common measure of 62 and 107-1*62. Lather, rinse, repeat. In the third column we accumulate x and y factors .*

At the last algorithm iteration, it is concluded that the values $x=11$ and $y=19$ satisfy the equation.

Is this the only solution? Certainly not. Consider:

$$62 \cdot 107 - 107 \cdot 62 = 0$$

Add it to:

$$11 \cdot 107 - 19 \cdot 62 = 0$$

And the result

$$(11+62) \cdot 107 - (19+107) \cdot 62 = 0$$

which implies another solution of $x=73$, $y=126$! Fortunately, we know that x (i.e. *a22*) and y (i.e. *a12*) has to be smaller than 62 (i.e. *a21*) and 107 (i.e. *a11*), correspondingly. Therefore they can be dismissed.

The most important implication of the research in this section is that the combination of *a11* with *a21* is always unique. We can go as far as reducing the MatrixTreeNodes definition to these two attributes (and calculate the other two columns on the fly via extended Euclidean algorithm), or leave the redundant attributes in the table and just declare the unique key. The second alternative is chosen, which is justified by the next step. Knowing that *a12* and *a22* are always negative, we are going to store their absolute values. Then, as been shown already, the child values *a12* and *a22* have to refer to some parent identified by *a11* and *a21*. In other words, a child always refers to its parent explicitly via the *foreign key* constraint.

Therefore, the tree schema design is enhanced as shown below:

```
table MatrixTreeNodes (
    a11 integer,
    a12 integer,
    a21 integer,
    a22 integer
);

alter table MatrixTreeNodes
ADD CONSTRAINT uk_node UNIQUE (a11,a21)
ADD CONSTRAINT fk_adjacency FOREIGN KEY (a12,a22)
            REFERENCES MatrixTreeNodes (a11,a21);
```

The hierarchy design in which a node refers to the parent name explicitly is called the *adjacency* tree model, and its scope is actually bigger than trees. The schema for the adjacency model is the following:

```
table AdjacentTreeNodes (
    id integer,
    parent_id integer
);

alter table AdjacentTreeNodes
ADD CONSTRAINT uk_node UNIQUE (id)
ADD CONSTRAINT fk_adjacency FOREIGN KEY (parent_id)
            REFERENCES AdjacentTreeNodes (id);
```

Unlike matrix encoding, there is no theory regarding how to choose a set of node identifiers, except for the obvious restrictions that the *id* column is a unique identifier, and *parent_id* always refers to the parent node. The general adjacency model is the main topic of the next chapter.

There is one subtle distinction between matrix and adjacency encodings. What the root node refers to. In adjacency encoding the root node *parent_id* has to be NULL, as there is no parent. In the matrix encoding the extended Euclidean algorithm is simply applied and the four numbers obtained. The root node refers to some nonexistent parent! What if the root node matrix encoding:

$$\begin{bmatrix} 1 & -1 \\ 1 & 0 \end{bmatrix}$$

is changed into:

$$\begin{bmatrix} 1 & null \\ 1 & null \end{bmatrix}$$

Technically, NULLS cannot be forced into the matrix entries — they would destroy all the algorithms that were developed so far. It is more reasonable to admit that the formal referential constraint declaration for matrix encoding is invalid, and therefore, should be retracted from the schema design. This is not a big issue, however, given that matrix encoding enjoys more sophisticated constraints than referential integrity.

Parent is NULL?

In the adjacency model the root node refers to the NULL parent. Does it mean that the query "Find the root node's parent" cannot be answered? In the matrix model the root refers to the imaginary parent, and the query "Find the root node's parent" returns the empty set as it supposed to.

Once again, it was possible to establish direct links between parent and children because the values of *a12* and *a22* were negated. From now on, the generic matrix node encoding will be referred to as:

$$\begin{bmatrix} a_{11} & -a_{12} \\ a_{21} & -a_{22} \end{bmatrix}$$

Now that the informal referential integrity constraint is available, querying parent and children nodes becomes obvious.

Find all the employees who report directly to Jones.

```
select child.name
from MatrixTreeNodes parent, MatrixTreeNodes child
where parent.name = 'Jones'
and child.a11 = parent.a12 and child.a21 = parent.a22
```

Who is Jones' manager?

```
select parent.name
from MatrixTreeNodes parent, MatrixTreeNodes child
where child.name = 'Jones'
and child.a11 = parent.a12 and child.a21 = parent.a22
```

Nested Intervals

Querying descendants has to be done via nested intervals. Given the matrix

$$\begin{bmatrix} a_{11} & -a_{12} \\ a_{21} & -a_{22} \end{bmatrix}$$

the interval boundaries are calculated as:

$$\frac{a_{11}}{a_{21}}, \frac{a_{11} - a_{12}}{a_{21} - a_{22}}$$

Of these two numbers which is interval is lower bound and which is the upper bound? Let's compare them. Multiplying both numbers to the product of their denominators and simplifying the result, the problem is reduced to answering if

$$0 < a_{11} a_{22} - a_{12} a_{21}$$

Here is the determinant expression, again, which evaluates to 1. Hence, interval boundaries are ordered as:

$$\frac{a_{11}}{a_{21}} < \frac{a_{11} - a_{12}}{a_{21} - a_{22}}$$

Next, how can we be sure those intervals are indeed nested? Let's compare an arbitrary node interval ends with that of its children. The *nth* child interval encoding is:

$$\begin{bmatrix} a_{11} & -a_{12} \\ a_{21} & -a_{22} \end{bmatrix} \cdot \begin{bmatrix} n+1 & -1 \\ 1 & 0 \end{bmatrix} = \begin{bmatrix} a_{11}(n+1) - a_{12} & -a_{11} \\ a_{21}(n+1) - a_{22} & -a_{21} \end{bmatrix}$$

Therefore, the child interval boundaries are:

$$\frac{a_{11}(n+1) - a_{12}}{a_{21}(n+1) - a_{22}}, \frac{a_{11} n - a_{12}}{a_{21} n - a_{22}}$$

Note, that the second endpoint is the same expression as the first one, with *n* decremented by *1*. Therefore, the following must be checked for any $n \geq 1$

$$\frac{a_{11}}{a_{21}} \leq \frac{a_{11} n - a_{12}}{a_{21} n - a_{22}}, \frac{a_{11} n - a_{12}}{a_{21} n - a_{22}} \leq \frac{a_{11} - a_{12}}{a_{21} - a_{22}}$$

Both inequalities reduce to

$$0 \leq a_{11} a_{22} - a_{12} a_{21}, 0 \leq n(a_{11} a_{22} - a_{12} a_{21})$$

correspondingly. This proves that the parent node interval indeed contains its child interval.

The second property of nested intervals – sibling node intervals being disjoint – can be proved in a similar fashion.

Descendants Query

Now that the nested intervals structure has been covered, querying the node's descendants can be looked at. As a first approximation, let's take the descendants query in terms of nested sets as a template and rewrite it in terms of nested intervals:

```
select descendant.*
from MatrixTreeNodes descendant, MatrixTreeNodes node
where descendant.a11/descendant.a21 between node.a11/node.a21
                 and (node.a11-node.a12)/(node.a21-node.a22)
and node.name = …  -- predicate uniquely identifying a node
```

Unfortunately, this query would produce a wrong result. None of the database vendors support the rational number datatype[50]. The ratios of integers would be silently casted into float numbers with accompanying errors due to lack of precision. All the expressions must be rewritten with divisions within the means of integer arithmetic:

```
select descendant.*
from MatrixTreeNodes descendant, MatrixTreeNodes node
where descendant.a11*node.a21 >= descendant.a21*node.a11
and   descendant.a11*node.a22 >= descendant.a21*node.a12
and node.name = …  -- predicate identifying a node uniquely
```

When the descendant query performance was explained in the context of nested sets, the index range scan was emphasized as an efficient way to extract all the descendant nodes. This idea generalizes to nested intervals, although interval boundaries must be indexed. Let's enhance the tree encoding schema design with two function-based indexes:

---

[50] In fact, rational datatype is not even part of SQL standard.

```
table MatrixTreeNodes (
   a11 integer,
   a12 integer,
   a21 integer,
   a22 integer
);

CREATE INDEX idx_left ON MatrixTreeNodes(a11/a21);
CREATE INDEX idx_right ON MatrixTreeNodes((a11-a12)/(a21-a22));
```

The query must be rewritten in such a way that the optimizer can leverage these indexes:

```
select descendant.*
from MatrixTreeNodes descendant, MatrixTreeNodes node
where descendant.a11*node.a21 >= descendant.a21*node.a11
and    descendant.a11*node.a22 >= descendant.a21*node.a12
and    descendant.a11/descendant.a21
       between node.a11/node.a21 - 0.0000001
       and (node.a11-node.a12)/(node.a21-node.a22) + 0.0000001
and node.name = …  -- predicate uniquely identifying a node
```

The constant *0.0000001* is designed to compensate for floating point arithmetic rounding errors. It essentially is a minimal supported mantissa. Please refer to your favorite database SQL manual in order to find the exact value. This way the index range scan would capture all the nodes in the interval, and possibly, some extra[51], and the small list of nodes is filtered with the exact condition.

Ancestor Criteria

Suppose there are two nodes: one encoded with matrix A, and the other encoded with B. Node A is an ancestor of B if and only if there is a directed path from A to B. In matrix terms, there has to be a sequence of atomic matrices so that after A is multiplied to it, matrix B *is then obtained*. By matrix multiplication associativity law, all those atomic matrices can be combined into a single matrix X. In other words, node A is an ancestor of node B if there is matrix X such that:

$$A X = B$$

---

[51] But not too many extra!

If matrix A has inverse A^{-1}, then when multiplying both sides to A^{-1} the result is:

$$X = A^{-1} B$$

The formula for the inverse of the 2×2 matrix is

$$\begin{bmatrix} a_{11} & -a_{12} \\ a_{21} & -a_{22} \end{bmatrix}^{-1} = \begin{bmatrix} -a_{22} & a_{12} \\ -a_{21} & a_{11} \end{bmatrix}$$

where knowledge was leveraged that the matrices always have a determinant 1. Therefore, given any nodes *A* and *B*, matrix *X* that encodes the path between them can always be found.

This is absurd, as node *B* might not be a descendant of *A*! Let's examine the phenomenon more closely. As usual, an example might be handy. Consider the nodes *A=1.7* and *B=1.3.2.5* in matrix encoding:

$$\begin{bmatrix} 2 & -1 \\ 1 & 0 \end{bmatrix} \cdot \begin{bmatrix} 8 & -1 \\ 1 & 0 \end{bmatrix} = \begin{bmatrix} 15 & -2 \\ 8 & -1 \end{bmatrix}$$

$$\begin{bmatrix} 2 & -1 \\ 1 & 0 \end{bmatrix} \cdot \begin{bmatrix} 4 & -1 \\ 1 & 0 \end{bmatrix} \cdot \begin{bmatrix} 3 & -1 \\ 1 & 0 \end{bmatrix} \cdot \begin{bmatrix} 6 & -1 \\ 1 & 0 \end{bmatrix} = \begin{bmatrix} 107 & -19 \\ 62 & -11 \end{bmatrix}$$

Then, A^{-1}B evaluates to:

$$\begin{bmatrix} 17 & -3 \\ 74 & -13 \end{bmatrix}$$

This is not a valid matrix encoding, however. It violates the constraint that the entries in the upper row are greater than the ones in the lower row.

Here is more detailed explanation for why this is happening. Since matrix *A* is decomposed into a product of (atomic) matrices, why not leverage *the law of inverse of matrix product*:

$$(P\,Q)^{-1} = Q^{-1}\,P^{-1}$$

In the example:

$$\left(\begin{bmatrix} 2 & -1 \\ 1 & 0 \end{bmatrix} \cdot \begin{bmatrix} 8 & -1 \\ 1 & 0 \end{bmatrix}\right)^{-1} = \begin{bmatrix} 8 & -1 \\ 1 & 0 \end{bmatrix}^{-1} \begin{bmatrix} 2 & -1 \\ 1 & 0 \end{bmatrix}^{-1}$$

Hence, A-1B expands into the following product of atomic matrices and their inverses

$$\begin{bmatrix} 8 & -1 \\ 1 & 0 \end{bmatrix}^{-1} \begin{bmatrix} 2 & -1 \\ 1 & 0 \end{bmatrix}^{-1} \begin{bmatrix} 2 & -1 \\ 1 & 0 \end{bmatrix} \begin{bmatrix} 4 & -1 \\ 1 & 0 \end{bmatrix} \begin{bmatrix} 3 & -1 \\ 1 & 0 \end{bmatrix} \begin{bmatrix} 6 & -1 \\ 1 & 0 \end{bmatrix}$$

where

$$\begin{bmatrix} 2 & -1 \\ 1 & 0 \end{bmatrix}^{-1} \begin{bmatrix} 2 & -1 \\ 1 & 0 \end{bmatrix}$$

collapses into the identity matrix. This is because both A=.1.7 and B=.1.3.2.5 start with the same prefix .1. Therefore, the above expression for A^{-1}B simplifies to

$$\begin{bmatrix} 8 & -1 \\ 1 & 0 \end{bmatrix}^{-1} \begin{bmatrix} 4 & -1 \\ 1 & 0 \end{bmatrix} \begin{bmatrix} 3 & -1 \\ 1 & 0 \end{bmatrix} \begin{bmatrix} 6 & -1 \\ 1 & 0 \end{bmatrix}$$

which cannot be further reduced. It is the multiplication by an atomic matrix inverse that violates the constraint.

In order to carry over this idea to SQL, A^{-1}B must be written in a generic form

$$\begin{bmatrix} -a_{22} & a_{12} \\ -a_{21} & a_{11} \end{bmatrix} \cdot \begin{bmatrix} b_{11} & -b_{12} \\ b_{21} & -b_{22} \end{bmatrix} = \begin{bmatrix} b_{21}\,a_{12} - b_{11}\,a_{22} & b_{12}\,a_{22} - b_{22}\,a_{12} \\ -b_{11}\,a_{21} + b_{21}\,a_{11} & -b_{22}\,a_{11} + b_{12}\,a_{21} \end{bmatrix}$$

which translates to the descendants query from the previous section:

```
select B.*
from MatrixTreeNodes A, MatrixTreeNodes B
where B.a21*A.a12 - B.a11*A.a22 > -B.a11*A.a21 + B.a21*A.a11
and   B.a12*A.a22 - B.a22*A.a12 > -B.a22*A.a11 + B.a12*A.a21
and A.name = …  -- predicate identifying a node uniquely
```

Admittedly, this query is slightly more complicated than the nested intervals version. The real contribution of this section is introducing inverse matrices, which will be leveraged later when relocating subtrees.

Ancestors Query

Logically, finding all the ancestors can be accomplished by swapping the roles of the two join operands in the descendants query. Once again, such a query will not be a good performer. In the section on materialized path encoding the problem was split into two parts: computing all the node encodings in the chain first, and extracting all the nodes by those keys from the database, second. Since a close tie between the materialized path and matrix encoding was introduced earlier, it would come as no surprise that we can perform the same trick with matrices.

Let's look into matrix encodings of parent and child nodes one more time:

$$\begin{bmatrix} a_{11} & -a_{12} \\ a_{21} & -a_{22} \end{bmatrix} \cdot \begin{bmatrix} n+1 & -1 \\ 1 & 0 \end{bmatrix} = \begin{bmatrix} a_{11}(n+1) - a_{12} & -a_{11} \\ a_{21}(n+1) - a_{22} & -a_{21} \end{bmatrix}$$

The child just inherited the entries a_{11} and a_{21} from its parent. Therefore, to calculate the left row entries of the parent, just take them from the right row of the child matrix. The right row elements are the remainders of the division of the parent left row by the right row, and as an added bonus, the sibling order number n was obtained.

Let's demonstrate it on the familiar example of child node 1.3.2.5:

$$\begin{bmatrix} 107 & -19 \\ 62 & -11 \end{bmatrix}$$

The modulo function calculates the remainders:

$$19\text{-mod}(107,19) = 7$$
$$11\text{-mod}(62,11) = 4$$

Let's double check the results:

$$107 = (5+1)*19 - 7$$
$$62 = (5+1)*11- 4$$

Hence, the parent encoding:

$$\begin{bmatrix} 19 & -7 \\ 11 & -4 \end{bmatrix}$$

This process continues as to find the grandfather:

$$\begin{bmatrix} 7 & -2 \\ 4 & -1 \end{bmatrix}$$

And to find the grand grandfather:

$$\begin{bmatrix} 2 & -1 \\ 1 & 0 \end{bmatrix}$$

which happens to be the root – a matrix with $a_{22} = 0$. Now that we have a list of ancestor matrices, how are they extracted from database? One solution would be by building a dynamic query like this:

```
select *
from MatrixTreeNodes
where a11=19 and a12=7 and a21=11 and a22=4
   or a11=7 and a12=2 and a21=4 and a22=1
   or a11=2 and a12=1 and a21=1 and a22=0
```

Though a better approach would be storing the ancestor encoding in a temporary Ancestors table, and using the generic query:

```
select n.*
from MatrixTreeNodes n, Ancestors a
where n.a11=a.a11 and n.a12=a.a12 and n.a21=a.a21 and n.a22=a.a22
```

Some RDBMS engines allow programming table functions so that the table of ancestor encodings can be produced as an output of such a function. Syntactically, the query would become:

```
select n.*
from MatrixTreeNodes n, Table(Ancestors(49,9,38,7)) a
where n.a11=a.a11 and n.a12=a.a12 and n.a21=a.a21 and n.a22=a.a22
```

Given the entries $a_{11}=107$, $a_{12}=19$, $a_{21}=62$, and $a_{22}=11$, the Ancestors table function is supposed to calculate the chain of ancestor encodings.

Converting Matrix to Path

The previous section revealed the identity connecting parent and child encoding

$$\begin{bmatrix} a_{11} & -a_{12} \\ a_{21} & -a_{22} \end{bmatrix} \cdot \begin{bmatrix} n+1 & -1 \\ 1 & 0 \end{bmatrix} = \begin{bmatrix} a_{11}(n+1) - a_{12} & -a_{11} \\ a_{21}(n+1) - a_{22} & -a_{21} \end{bmatrix}$$

and mentioned that a sibling order number n is a remainder of integer division *floor((a11*(n+1)-a12)/a12)*. In our example, the node 1.3.2.5 is the 5th children of the node 1.3.2:

$$\text{floor}(107/19) = 5$$
$$\text{floor}(62/11) = 5$$

Working all the way to the root, the other numbers in the path can be found.

The path is generated in the order from the leaf to the root. Perhaps, it would be more convenient to generate it in the opposite order. The procedure is essentially the same, but applied to the transposed matrix.

Inserting Nodes

So far our attention was on queries. But how is the tree filled with nodes? The new node location is unambiguously defined by the node's parent and the node's position among the other children. Normally, given a parent, a new node is attached as the youngest child. Therefore, the node's insertion is accomplished in two steps:

1. Query all the immediate children and find the oldest child

```
select max(floor(a11/a12)) as N from MatrixTreeNodes
where a11 = :parent_a12
and a21 = :parent_a22
```

where *:parent_a12* and *:parent_a22* are the host variables of the parent node encoding.

2. Insert the node at the *n*-th position:

```
insert into MatrixTreeNodes (a11,a12,a21,a22) values
(:parent_a11*(:N+1) - :parent_a12,
 :parent_a11,
 :parent_a21*(:N+1) - :parent_a22,
 :parent_a21);
```

These two steps can be combined into a single *insert as select* statement.

Relocating Tree Branches

This is the section where matrix algebra really shines. Consider a tree branch located at the node encoded with matrix A, and suppose it is to be moved to the new location under node B. How would the encoding of some node C (which is located in the tree branch under A) change?

That is quite an easy task for materialized path encoding. First, find the path from the node A to C. Then, append it to node B. This idea transfers to matrices almost literally. The encoding of node C is a product of its ancestor A and some other matrix:

$$A X = C$$

Matrix X corresponds to the path from A to C. This path is appended to path B; the matrices are multiplied and thus the resulting encoding obtained is:

$$B X$$

The unknown matrix X is calculated via inverse matrix, so the final answer is:

$$B A^{-1} C$$

In order to translate this into SQL, the answer is expanded component-wise:

$$\begin{bmatrix} b_{11} & -b_{12} \\ b_{21} & -b_{22} \end{bmatrix} \cdot \begin{bmatrix} -a_{22} & a_{12} \\ -a_{21} & a_{11} \end{bmatrix} \cdot \begin{bmatrix} c_{11} & -c_{12} \\ c_{21} & -c_{22} \end{bmatrix} =$$

$$[(-b_{11} a_{22} + b_{12} a_{21}) c_{11} + (b_{11} a_{12} - b_{12} a_{11}) c_{21},$$
$$-(-b_{11} a_{22} + b_{12} a_{21}) c_{12} - (b_{11} a_{12} - b_{12} a_{11}) c_{22}]$$
$$[(-b_{21} a_{22} + b_{22} a_{21}) c_{11} + (b_{21} a_{12} - b_{22} a_{11}) c_{21},$$
$$-(-b_{21} a_{22} + b_{22} a_{21}) c_{12} - (b_{21} a_{12} - b_{22} a_{11}) c_{22}]$$

And can be coded in SQL as:

```
update MatrixTreeNodes c
set c.all = (:b12*:a21-:b11*:a22)*c.all
          +(:b11*:a12-:b12*:a11)*c.a21
    c.a12 = (:b12*:a21-:b11*:a22)*c.a12
          +(:b11*:a12-:b12*:a11)*c.a22
    c.a21 = (:b22*:a21-:b21*:a22)*c.all
          +(:b21*:a12-:b22*:a11)*c.a21
    c.a22 = (:b22*:a21-:b21*:a22)*c.a12
          +(:b21*:a12-:b22*:a11)*c.a22
where c.all*:a21 >= c.a21*:all  -- all the descendants of matrix
and   c.all*:a22 >= c.a21*:a12  -- [[:all,:a12][:a21,:a22]]
```

Ordering

So far emphasis has been placed on how to query the tree structure in various encodings. The presentation layer often demands an ordered output. The difficulty here is that the end user is expected to specify some ordering criteria on runtime, and the order might be nonconforming to the order encoded in the tree structure. For example, consider a familiar hierarchy or employees with nested sets encoding:

ENAME	LEFT	RIGHT
⊟ KING	1	20
⊟ JONES	2	7
⊟ SCOTT	3	6
⊟ ADAMS	4	5
⊟ FORD	8	11
⊟ SMITH	9	10
⊟ BLAKE	12	19
⊟ ALLEN	13	14
⊟ WARD	15	16
⊟ MARTIN	17	18

The tree is effectively ordered by the *LEFT* column. A user might ask to display it locally, ordered by the employee names at each hierarchy level. It is easy to see that the global ordering criteria is essentially the path from the root to a node, which is made of concatenated names:

ENAME	PATH
⊟ KING	KING
⊟ BLAKE	KING.BLAKE
⊟ ALLEN	KING.BLAKE.ALLEN
⊟ MARTIN	KING.BLAKE.MARTIN
⊟ WARD	KING.BLAKE.WARD
⊟ JONES	KING.JONES
⊟ FORD	KING.JONES.FORD
⊟ SMITH	KING.JONES.FORD.SMITH
⊟ SCOTT	KING.JONES.SCOTT
⊟ ADAMS	KING.JONES.SCOTT.ADAMS

Unlike the materialized path, the path of concatenated names must be generated dynamically. The technical problem here is aggregating the names into a path string. Fortunately, in Chapter 3 the *LIST* aggregate function was explained. Therefore, the process continues by taking the familiar nested sets query, which returns a list of all node ancestors, and aggregating those lists into paths:

```
SELECT ii.left
       ,CONCAT_LIST(CAST( COLLECT('.'||i.ename) AS strings )) path
FROM   Employees i, Employees ii
where ii.left between i.left and i.right
group by ii.left;
```

On a cautious note, this particular implementation of the *LIST* aggregate is agnostic of the order of the aggregation summands. The reader must double check that his favorite string concatenation method concatenates summands in the right order.

Ordering by dynamic path seems to be a natural solution until we are asked to order by numeric criteria, salary, for example. Numbers sorted as strings go in the wrong order. They have to be padded. The other concern is that of negative values. All these inconveniences make the dynamic path solution unsatisfactory.

An alternative solution is recreating the hierarchy dynamically with the structure, which is conforming to the required ordering. At first thought, recreating the hierarchy smells performance problems, but our rationale hinges upon a typical usage scenario. It must be the GUI that wants to display the ordered hierarchy, and GUI rendering capabilities impose common sense limits on the tree size. Even if the GUI were able to display the whole tree, an end user would be overwhelmed by the volume of information that he were presented "at once". It is fair to assume that a reasonably designed GUI would display only a local portion of the hierarchy, no matter how big the whole hierarchy might be.

Therefore, the issue of hierarchy ordering should be considered within the scope of application design. The application programmer designs a method of hierarchy navigation and display, which guarantees that the GUI displays only a small part of the hierarchy. A familiar example is an organizational chart where no more than two levels of the hierarchy are displayed at each tree node: employee subordinates, and his supervisor. Ordering such a puny tree is a laughably easy exercise for a reader who has advanced thus far in this book.

An alternative design is a dynamic tree widget where each node exists in on of the two states: expanded or collapsed. The Windows file manager utility is a typical example. In principle, a directory tree could be expanded fully, but it is unreasonable to expect that there is a user who is up to the challenge of manually expanding a hierarchy of any significant size to the full depth.

Exotic Labeling Schemas

The tree encoding area is flourishing with various methods. It is so easy to invent yet another tree labeling schema! This contrasts to general graphs, which appear to defy encoding ideas. This section reviews others, arguably, less practical tree encoding methods.

Dietz Encoding

One natural way to label a tree is the pre-order traversal as shown in Figure 5.10.

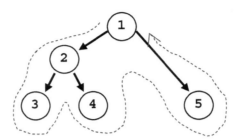

Figure 5.10 - *Pre-order traversal.*

It is natural because the tree nodes are indexed in the depth-first order, and tree node records are in the depth-first order in a nearly ubiquitous tree display with the levels laid out horizontally:

Employee Name	Preorder#
⊟ KING	1
⊟ JONES	2
⊟ SCOTT	3
⊟ ADAMS	4
⊟ FORD	5
⊟ SMITH	6
⊟ BLAKE	7
⊟ ALLEN	8
⊟ WARD	9
⊟ MARTIN	10

The post-order traversal is a less intuitive way of navigating a tree. The nodes are visited in the same order, but the node's index number assignment is postponed until all of the node's children are indexed:

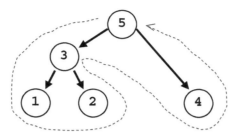

Figure 5.11 - *Post-order traversal.*

The Dietz tree encoding assigns a pair of indexes: *preorder#, postorder#* to each node.

It is immediate that the Dietz tree encoding is volatile. Inserting a new node disrupts existing encodings, both pre-order and post-order.

Querying the Dietz encoded tree is based upon the following ancestor criteria. Node *x* is an ancestor of *y* if and only if *x.preorder#* $\leq$ *y.preorder#* and *y.postorder#* $\leq$ *x.postorder#*. This criteria appears to be identical to that of nested intervals, although unlike nested intervals neither *preorder#* < *postorder#*, nor *preorder#* < *postorder#* is universally true for all the nodes.

Figure 5.12 is a two-dimensional picture of Dietz encoding. It is assumed that *preorder#* is the horizontal axis, and *postorder#* is the vertical axis.

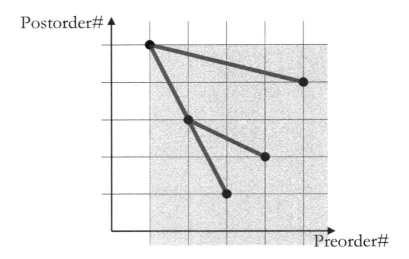

Figure 5.12 - *Two dimensional view of Dietz encoding. A root node preorder#=1, postorder#=5 has all it's descendants within the cone preorder#>1, postorder#<5.*

Each node x has its descendant nodes y bounded within the two-dimensional cone defined by the two inequalities $x.preorder\# \leq y.preorder\#$ and $y.postorder\# \leq x.postorder\#$. For nested intervals we would additionally have $preorder\# < postorder\#$ or in geometric terms have all the nodes above the diagonal $preorder\# = postorder\#$. If all the tree nodes are moved above the diagonal somehow, then the Dietz encoding would be transformed into nested intervals. Linear mapping

$$left = total\#nodes - postorder\# +1$$
$$right = 2 \cdot total\#nodes - preorder\#$$

achieves that goal in Figure 5.13.

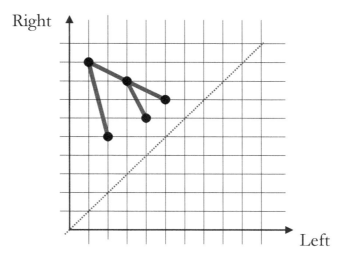

Right

Left

Figure 5.13- *Dietz encoding linearly transformed to have all the tree nodes above the main diagonal – to nested interval encoding.*

Pre-order – Depth Encoding

Yet another way to label the tree is storing the combination of the pre-order index number and level. Let's glance over the basic queries, though.

- To find the node's parent, select all the nodes on the upper level, filter out all the nodes beneath, and choose the one with maximum *preorder#* among the rest. In the familiar example

Employee Name	Preorder#
⊟ KING	1
⊟ JONES	2
⊟ SCOTT	3
⊟ ADAMS	4
⊟ FORD	5
⊟ SMITH	6
⊟ BLAKE	7
⊟ ALLEN	8
⊟ WARD	9
⊟ MARTIN	10

Smith's parent is searched for among the upper level nodes: *Scott, Ford, Allen, Ward* and *Martin*. *Allen, Ward* and *Martin* are rejected as they all have a *preorder#* greater than *Smith*. Among *Scott* and *Ford* the latter has a greater *preorder#*.

- To find all the descendants, locate the next node on the same level and the next node on the parent level, choose the closest of the two, and select all the nodes between the given node and the chosen one.

  For Scott, pick up Ford and Blake, then select every node between Scott and Ford (exclusively).

- Finding all the node's children is just filtering out of case #2 the nodes with the proper level.

- Finding a path to the root is simply selecting all the predecessor nodes, grouping them by level, and extracting the maximum sequence numbers per each group.

This is, again, volatile encoding, which kills our further interest in detailed exploration.

Reversed Nesting

Let's revise the nested sets example in Figure 5.2. This time instead of a parent set containing its children sets, we demand the parent set to be contained in its children as shown in Figure 5.14.

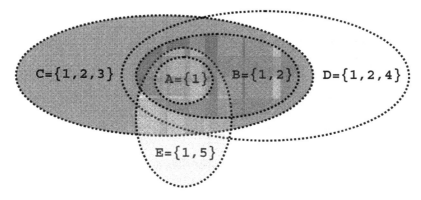

Figure 5.14 - *Nested sets structure for the tree in fig. 5.2a with set containment reversed. Now, a child set is required to contain its parent.*

This variation of Nested Sets encoding is non-volatile. Once again, there is no direct support of the set datatype on most platforms, so we have to find a workaround. Armed with Boolean algebra each set is represented as a Boolean vector, the latter can be stored as plain strings. For example, $\{0,1,4,6\}$ becomes '*1100101*'.

In general, set containment does not correspond to any standard operation on strings. However, sets of tree nodes are special as shown in Figure 5.15.

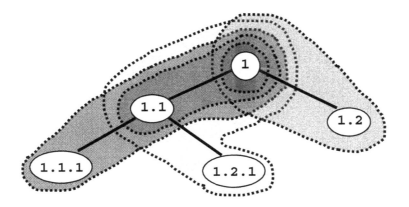

Figure 5.15 - *A different view of the reverse nested sets structure for the tree in fig. 5.14. A set is indistinguishable from path to the root.*

Set elements correspond to tree nodes, and each set is associated with a path from the root to a node. Hence, the set containment for reverse nested sets is the same as the substring operation. The methods for querying materialized path encoded trees must work for reverse nested sets as well.

Roji Thomas suggested yet another tree encoding, which is closely related to the reverse nested sets. In his method each node is labeled in two steps. First, each node is designated a unique prime number. Then, each node is encoded with a number, a product of the primes on the path from the node to the root. Node A is ancestor of node B whenever the encoding of A divides B.

By the fundamental theorem of arithmetic, every integer has a unique prime factorization:

$$ N = 2^{\alpha_1} \cdot 3^{\alpha_2} \cdot 5^{\alpha_3} \cdot \ldots \cdot p_k^{\alpha_k} $$

It is immediate that the vector of prime orders $(\alpha_1, \alpha_2, \alpha_3, \ldots, \alpha_k)$ in Roji Thomas' case is Boolean, and his encoding is essentially reverse nested sets. Without establishing this connection the investigation would not be complete.

When studying any encoding schema, it is natural to start with the *expressive power*, verifying that any hierarchical query can be expressed in terms of new encoding. The second concern is efficiency, with emphasis on access path via index. It might not be obvious how to index tree nodes in Roji Thomas encoding, yet it is the connection to reverse nested sets that solves the problem.

Ordered Partitions

Given a positive integer N, in how many ways it can be expressed as a sum of smaller integers? Assume the order of the summands is important. Although this problem seems to be too distant from database practice, it nevertheless leads to yet another encoding method.

First of all, ordered integer partition is essentially a materialized path. Let's enumerate all possible partitions by arranging them into the following table:

Encoding	Partition	N
1	1	1
2	1+1	2
3	2	2
4	1+1+1	3
5	1+2	3
6	2+1	3
7	3	3
8	1+1+1+1	4
9	1+1+2	4
10	1+2+1	4
11	1+3	4
12	2+1+1	4
13	2+2	4
14	3+1	4
15	4	4
16	1+1+1+1+1	5

This enumeration is generated recursively. All the partitions of N+1 are generated from the partitions of N in either way:

- putting an extra component with 1 in front of all of the other components of N, or

- incrementing the first component of each partition of N by *1*.

Then, it follows that partitions encoded with the even numbers have 1 as the last component. Indeed, as long as partitions of N have been evenly encoded to end up with 1, this property is carried over to the partitions of $N+1$. Since partitions are associated with materialized paths, this means the oldest child encoding is twice that of the parent!

For odd encodings, let's decrement them by *1*, first. This would produce an even encoding – the case that we have studied already. Compared to the former odd encoded partition, the latter even encoded partition has an extra component – the trailing *1*. Both are partitions of the same number N, however. This can be achieved only if the last component of the odd encoding is the sum of the last component and the last but one component of the even encoding. For example, the partition encoded as *11*, i.e. *1+3*, has the last component *3* to be represented as *2+1* in the partition number *10*, i.e. *1+2+1*. Then, by halving the even encoding, the encoding of the younger sibling (relative to the original odd encoded node) will be obtained!

Although these discoveries allow defining an ancestor relation which could serve as a basis for hierarchical queries, performance is still important. It is unclear if the integer partition based encoding schema admits an efficient querying of the node's descendants. Once again, our benchmark is nested intervals encoding, where all the descendants can be accessed via index range scan. It turns out that integer partition encoding is very closely related to nested intervals encoding with dyadic rational numbers; in fact, there is a transparent mapping between them. I will not pursue this venue here any longer; however I will refer an interested reader to a series of my papers published by *dbazine.com*. Once more, from a practical perspective Farey fractions provide a more economical opportunity to organize a system of nested intervals.

Case Study: Homegrown C Function Call Profiler

Profiler is a common tool for performance analysis. It determines how long certain parts of the program takes to execute, how often those parts are executed, and then generates a tree (or graph) of function calls. Typically this information is used to identify the portions of the program that takes the longest to complete. Then, the time consuming parts are expected to be optimized to run faster.

If the reader begins to suspect that there is plenty of tools doing the job, then (s)he's absolutely right. Those tools, however, are just programs. They build canned reports. We'll approach the problem from database centric angle. Let's place the profiling data into the database, and then we can query it any way we like!

First, the data must be gathered. Linux/Unix pstack is a primitive utility that does the job. The calls stack can be queried repeatedly with a shell script like this

```
integer i=0
while ((i <= 999));
do
  pstack -F 25672 | tee -a pstack.trc;
  (( i = i + 1));
done
```

where the magic number *25672* is the process number to attach to.

The output is streamed into a file with the content like this:

```
25672:        oracleEMR920U3 (DESCRIPTION=(LOCAL=YES)(ADDRESS=(PROTOCOL=beq)))
 009d5930 appdrv   (ffbe82d8, 180000, ffbe82d8, feb5e794, 0, ffbe8351)
 009fd85c kkofmx   (0, 0, 0, 0, fe7bebb4, 2a38a43e) + 624
 009f834c kkonxc   (fe7bebb4, fe4b3124, …) + 8c
 009fc65c kkotap   (200000, 0, 0, 0, 1, 4000) + 1444
 009f1154 kkojnp   (0, 0, 0, 0, 108, 0) + 14dc
 009ef9e8 kkocnp   (fe7bebb4, 1, 0, 0, 1f, 7c) + f0
 …
```

```
008f4b5c opidrv    (3c, 4, ffbef504, 2f6c6f67, 0, 2f) + 1ec
001d666c sou2o     (ffbef514, 3c, 4, ffbef504, 0, 0) + 10
001cf59c main      (2, ffbef5dc, ffbef5e8, 30d2000, 0, 0) + ec
001cf488 _start    (0, 0, 0, 0, 0, 0) + 108
25672:       oracleEMR920U3 (DESCRIPTION=(LOCAL=YES)(ADDRESS=(PROTOCOL=beq)))
00a1c6a4 kkorbp    (ffbe8e3c, 0, ffffffff, 0, 0, ffbe8e61) + 808
00a1f230 kkobrfak  (ffbe8e3c, ffbe8e60, fe39a42c, 0, 0, 1) + 8c
00a1d92c kkofbp    (2a3bef38, 0, 2a3bef38, 0, 0, 1) + 584
00a22ddc kkobmp    (10, fe4b39e4, 23, fe4df610, 0, fe4b3ac4) + bc
...
008f4b5c opidrv    (3c, 4, ffbef504, 2f6c6f67, 0, 2f) + 1ec
001d666c sou2o     (ffbef514, 3c, 4, ffbef504, 0, 0) + 10
001cf59c main      (2, ffbef5dc, ffbef5e8, 30d2000, 0, 0) + ec
001cf488 _start    (0, 0, 0, 0, 0, 0) + 108
25672:       oracleEMR920U3 (DESCRIPTION=(LOCAL=YES)(ADDRESS=(PROTOCOL=beq)))
00a1f218 kkobrf    (ffbe8e3c, ffbe8e60, 0, 0, 0, 0) + 74
00a1d690 kkofbp    (2a3bef38, 0, 2a3bef38, 0, 0, 1) + 2e8
00a22ddc kkobmp    (10, fe4b39e4, 23, fe4ff610, 0, fe4b3ac4) + bc
009fc678 kkotap    (200000, 0, 0, 0, 1, 4000) + 1460
...
```

The detailed file structure is not important. What is essential for this analysis is the sequence of the function calls (emphasized in bold) within each section (demarcated with italic delimiters). Specifically, we would like to move the data to the database with the following schema:

```
table function_sequences (
    stack_id integer,      -- section
    id       integer,      -- sequence #
    func     varchar2(100) -- function name
);
```

The sample data snippet is now a part of the database table:

```
select * from function_sequences
```

STACK_ID	ID	FUNC
1	1	appdrv
1	2	kkofmx
1	3	kkonxc
1	4	kkotap
1	5	kkojnp
1	6	kkocnp
...	...	...
1	28	opidrv
1	29	sou2o

1	30	main
1	31	_start
2	1	kkorbp
2	2	kkobrfak
2	3	kkofbp
2	4	kkobmp
...	...	...
2	30	sou2o
2	31	main
2	32	_start
3	1	kkobrfak
3	2	kkofbp
3	3	kkobmp
3	4	kkotap
...	...	...

The data mover implementation part is rather boring. The input file is read line by line. If the line starts with the magic number 25672, a section delimiter string is being parsed. Then, the *stack_id* counter is incremented, and the *id* counter initialized. Otherwise, the function name is read and the *id counter* incremented.

It was easy to implement the function *id*s increasing with each line scanned, but their order is inconsistent with stack slots numbering. It is convenient to re-label the functions so that the root function *_start* is always labeled with *id = 1*. The new view/table name – *Stacks* – reflects the fact that the data is now conventionally aligned with the stack data structure:

```
create table Stacks as
select s.stack_id id, height - s.id + 1 pos, func
   from function_sequences s, (
   select stack_id, max(id) height from function_sequences
   group by stack_id
) ss
where s.stack_id = ss.stack_id
;
```

We finally arrived to an interesting side of the problem, the reporting. How are all these stacks combined into a meaningful call graph? In particular, what defines the function location in the call graph? Having learned so much about materialized path encoding already, the answer will be hardly surprising. It is a path assembled from of all the names on the call stack that is being sought after.

Technically, functions are concatenated with the list[52] aggregate function:

```
select id, list('.'||func)
          over (partition by id order by pos) path,
       pos, func
from stacks;
```

ID	PATH	FUNC
1	._start	_start
1	._start.main	main
1	._start.main.sou2o	sou2o
1	._start.main.sou2o.opidrv	opidrv
1	...	kglobld
1	._start.main.sou2o.opidrv. ... .kkoqbc.kkooqb.kkocnp	kkocnp
1	._start.main.sou2o.opidrv. ... .kkoqbc.kkooqb.kkocnp.kkojnp	kkojnp
1	._start.main.sou2o.opidrv. ... .kkoqbc.kkooqb.kkocnp.kkojnp.kkotap	kkotap
1	._start.main.sou2o.opidrv. ... .kkoqbc.kkooqb.kkocnp.kkojnp.kkotap.kkonxc	kkonxc
1	._start.main.sou2o.opidrv. ... .kkoqbc.kkooqb.kkocnp.kkojnp.kkotap.kkonxc.kkofmx	kkofmx
1	._start.main.sou2o.opidrv. ... .kkoqbc.kkooqb.kkocnp.kkojnp.kkotap.kkonxc.kkofmx.appdrv	appdrv
2	._start	_start
2	._start.main	main
2	._start.main.sou2o	sou2o
2	._start.main.sou2o.opidrv	opidrv
2	...	opiodr

---

[52] To remind, the list string concatenation function were defined in the section dedicated to user-defined aggregates of chapter 3.

The materialized path can now be used to *group by* the stack tree nodes with the identical path together, and/or *order by* the nodes to get a nice indented tree layout:

```
select func, pos-1 depth, count(1) from (
  select id, list('.'||func)
            over (partition by id order by pos) path, pos, func
  from
  stacks
) group by path, pos, func
order by path;
```

FUNC	COUNT(1)
⊟ _start	632
⊟ main	632
⊟ sou2o	632
⊟ opidrv	632
⊟ opiodr	632
⊟ opiino	632
⊟ opitsk	632
⊟ opikndf2	79
⊟ nioqrc	79
⊟ nsdo	78
⊟ nsrdr	78
⊟ nsprecv	78
⊟ sntpread	78
⊟ read	78
⊟ nsdosend	1
⊟ nsdo	1
⊟ nsdofls	1
⊟ nspsend	1
⊟ _write	1
⊟ ttcpip	553
⊟ opiodr	553

The *count* aggregate is proportional to the time the execution has spent on this particular stack tree node. From there you would typically search for hotspot nodes, where a significant part of the execution time is spent.

Summary

- Nested Sets encoding is volatile and not efficient for finding the chain of the node's ancestors.

- The Stern-Brokot tree provides the most economical way to split intervals. This idea leads to matrix encoding.

- Matrix encoding combines the two models: adjacency relation and nested intervals. It is an especially appealing alternative to the materialized path encoding.

Exercises

Exercise 1:

Prove that in matrix encoding, sibling node intervals are disjointed.

Exercise 2:

It is very tempting to write the ancestors query like this:

```
select *
from MatrixTreeNodes
where a11 IN (19,7,2)
and a12 IN (7,2,1)
  and a21 IN (…,…,…)
  and a22 IN (…,…,…)
```

Explain why this query is flawed.

Exercise 3:

Implement the *Ancestors* table function in RDBMS of your choice.

Exercise 4:

Adapt the descendants query to return the list of the node's immediate children, that is

Select all the node's descendants, which are on the next level.

Compare it to the query that leverages the informal referential integrity constraint.

Exercise 5:

Combine the two matrix encoding node insertion steps into a single *insert as select* SQL statement.

Exercise 6:

Explore matrix encoding with atomic matrices of a kind:

$$\begin{bmatrix} n & 1 \\ 1 & 0 \end{bmatrix}$$

Exercise 7:

The atomic matrices from exercise 8 are *symmetric* -- they remain unchanged under transposition. Prove that the matrix transposition of the arbitrary node encoding corresponds to the inversed materialized path. (Then, symmetric matrix encoding corresponds to palindrome path!) Hint: *matrix transposition law:*

$$(A\,B)^T = B^T\,A^T$$

Exercise 8:

Explore matrix encoding with the atomic matrices of a kind:

$$\begin{bmatrix} n+1 & i \\ i & 0 \end{bmatrix}$$

Exercise 9:

Prove that the linear transformation of Dietz encoding indeed meets all the nested interval constraints.

Exercise 10:

Consider the chain of ancestors of node A, and the chain of ancestors of node B. Among their common ancestors exists the oldest one, which is called the *nearest common ancestor*. Write the nearest common ancestor query in the matrix tree encoding.

Graphs in SQL

Introduction

Graphs are much more challenging than trees. Even something as basic as a planar graph drawing is still an open research problem. There are few graph encodings and all of them are volatile. The set of graph problems is much richer and those problems are usually difficult. Applied to graphs the cowboy programmer attitude simply does not work.

This chapter will offer information regarding the different realms of graph methods: the recursive *with* kingdom, the *connect by* county, and the materialized transitive closure province. It will show typical graph queries, beginning with the number of connected components and ending with aggregated totals.

Schema Design

Being cautioned about the complexity of graph problems, this field should be approached carefully. Its thorough examination should begin with the schema design. When designing a schema, the first question to ask is how are graphs defined?

Graphs can be directed and undirected. This study is devoted almost exclusively to directed graphs; this is why the adjective is normally omitted. The directed graph definition is nearly ubiquitous.

Graph is a set of *nodes* connected by *edges*. Each edge is an ordered pair of nodes, to which are referred in this chapter as *head* and *tail*.

It is straightforward to carry over this graph definition to the schema design:

```
table Nodes (
    id integer primary key,
    ...
);

table Edges (
    head integer references Nodes,
    tail integer references Nodes,
    ...
);
```

Nodes and edges in a graph are normally weighted, hence the ellipsis in the schema definition. For example, in a network of cities connected by roads, each edge is labeled with the distance.

Tree Constraint

Representing trees as graphs is a very common database application programming practice. Consider the familiar *Emp* table:

```
select ename, empno, mgr from Emp
```

ENAME	EMPNO#	MGR#
⊟ KING	1	null
⊟ JONES	2	1
⊟ SCOTT	4	2
⊟ ADAMS	9	4
⊟ FORD	5	2
⊟ SMITH	10	5
⊟ BLAKE	3	1
⊟ ALLEN	6	3
⊟ WARD	7	3
⊟ MARTIN	8	3

Tree as Graph

In practice, tree schema design is often reduced to a single table

```
table Tree (
  id integer primary key,
  parentId integer references Tree,
  ...
);
```

This is just a sloppy programming style. The design with *Nodes* and *Edges* is clean – it separates the two concepts. With a single table it is easy to get confused when writing a hierarchical query. Also, consider the tree root node. It has to refer to $parentId = NULL$, whereas the design with Nodes and Edges does not require $NULL$s.

The most important concern, however, is that the graph schema, allows graphs which are not trees. Consider a cycle, for example:

head	tail
1	2
2	3
3	1

In order to describe a tree structure in graph terms, a couple of auxiliary definitions are needed.

- *Directed path* is a sequence of edges such that the previous edge head is the same as the next edge tail.

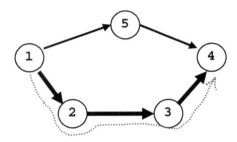

Figure 6.1 - *Graph with directed path (tail=1,head=2) (tail=2,head=3) (tail=3, head=4) emphasized.*

- *Undirected path* is a sequence of edges such that the previous edge head or tail coincides with the next edge head or tail.

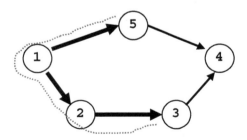

Figure 6.2 - *Graph with undirected path (tail=1,head=5) (tail=1,head=2) (tail=2,head=3) emphasized.*

An undirected path concept is needed to define a *connected graph* – a graph where there is a path between every pair of nodes. Otherwise, by *path* we would understand the directed path. For example, the graph in Figure 6.1 is connected.

Cycle is a closed path. In a closed path the last edge head is the same as the first edge tail. An *acyclic* graph does not contain cycles.

The tree definition, then, is essentially a constrained graph.

Tree as Subclass of Graph

Tree is an acyclic connected graph such that any two edges have distinct heads.

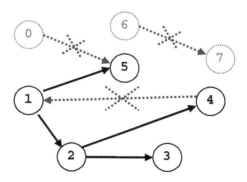

Figure 6.3 - *Tree constraints. The edge (tail=4,head=1) violates the acyclic property. The edge (tail=6,head=7) makes the graph disconnected. The edge (tail=0,head=5) has the same head as (tail=1,head=5).*

While the condition that any two edges have distinct heads could be declared effortlessly as a unique key constraint on the *head* column, the other two constraints are tough. In Chapter 4 we studied many tricks which allowed to enforce complex constraints via materialized views. If there is any hope leveraging that approach for enforcing tree constraint, then we'd better figure out how to query cycles, and calculate a number of connected components in a graph, as well.

This does not look very promising. Therefore, we have to give up on enforcing tree constraint in a graph model. To be fair, though, only a minority of database application programmers would insist that enforcing tree constraint is a matter of life-or-death. More important issues are:

- How is a graph model queried?

- Are the query methods efficient?

Transitive Closure

There are several key graph concepts that would guide your intuition when writing queries on graphs:

- *Reflexive closure* of a graph is built by adding missing loops – edges with the same endpoints. Reflexive closure is expressed easily in SQL:

```
select head, tail from Edges -- original relation
union
select head, head from Edges -- extra loops
union
select tail, tail from Edges -- more loops
```

- *Symmetric closure* of a (directed) graph is built by adding an inversely oriented edge for each edge in the original graph. In SQL:

```
select head, tail from Edges -- original relation
union
select tail, head from Edges -- inverse arrows
```

- *Transitive closure* of a (directed) graph is generated by connecting edges into paths and creating a new edge with the tail being the beginning of the path and the head being the end. Unlike the previous two cases, a transitive closure cannot be expressed with bare SQL essentials – the select, project, and join relational algebra operators.

For now, let's assume that we know how to query transitive closure, and demonstrate armed with these definitions how some problems can be approached. Here is a puzzle from the comp.databases.oracle.misc forum:

Suppose I have a table that contains Account# & RelatedAccount# (among other things).

How could I use CONNECT BY & START WITH in a query to count relationships or families. For example, in

```
ACCT    REL_ACCT
Bob     Mary
Bob     Jane
Jane    Bob
Larry   Moe
Curly   Larry
```

there are 2 relationship sets (Bob,Mary,Jane & Larry,Moe,Curly). If I added

```
Curly   Jane
```

then there'd be only 1 larger family. Can I use CONNECT BY & START with to detect such relationships and count them? In my case I'd be willing to go any number of levels deep in the recursion.

By ignoring Oracle specific SQL keywords as inessential to the problem at hand and using proper graph terminology, the question can be formulated into just one line:

Find a number of connected components in a graph.

The *Connected component* of a graph is a set of nodes reachable from each other. A node is reachable from another node if there is an undirected path between them.

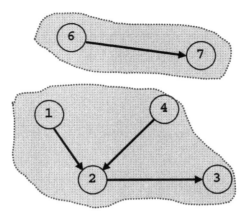

Figure 6.4 - *A graph with two connected components.*

Reachability is an equivalence relation: it is reflective, symmetric, and transitive. The reachability relation is obtained by closing the *Edges* relation to become reflective, symmetric, and transitive as shown in Figure 6.5.

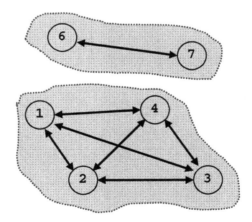

Figure 6.5 - *Reachability as an equivalence relation: graph from Figure 6.4 symmetrically and transitively closed.*

Now return to the problem of finding the number of connected components and assume that the reachability relation EquivalentNodess has already been calculated. Then, simply select the smallest node from each component. Informally this would read:

Select node(s) such that there is no node with smaller label reachable from it. Count them.

Formally:

```
select count(distinct tail) from EquivalentNodes e
where not exists (
    select * from EquivalentNodes ee
    where ee.head<e.tail and e.tail=ee.tail
);
```

Equivalence Relation and Group By (cont)

In one of the Chapter 1 sidebars we have attributed the incredible efficiency of the *group by* operator to its proximity to one of the most fundamental mathematical constructions – the equivalence relation. There are two ways to define an equivalence relation.

The first way is leveraging the existing equality operator on a domain of values. The second way is defining an equivalence relation explicitly, as a set of pairs. The standard *group by* operator is not able to understand an equivalence relation defined explicitly – this is the essence of the problem, which has just been solved.

Being able to query the number of connected components earned us an unexpected bonus: a connected graph can be redefined as a graph that has a single connected component. And, a connected graph with N nodes and $N-1$ edges must be a tree. Thus, counting nodes and edges together with a transitive closure is another opportunity to enforce tree constraint.

Transitive Closure

Now that some important graph closure properties have been established, everything is ready for transitive closure implementations. Unfortunately, this story has to branch here since database vendors approach the hierarchical query differently.

Recursive SQL

DB2 and SQL Server 2005 support the ANSI SQL standard recursive SQL, which renders the transitive closure effortlessly:

```
with TransClosedEdges (tail, head) as
( select tail, head from Edges
  union all
  select e.tail, ee.head from Edges e, TransClosedEdges ee
  where e.head = ee.tail
)
select distinct * from TransClosedEdges
```

This query looks artificial at first. It requires a certain educational background to fully appreciate it.

Consider the adjacency matrix of a graph. It is a square matrix with dimensions equal to the number of nodes. It is conventional to enumerate graph nodes with numbers from 1 to N, therefore, matching nodes with matrix columns and rows. With this arrangement matrix, entry a_{ij} naturally correspond to an edge from node i to node j. If there is indeed such an edge in a graph, then we define $a_{ij}=1$; otherwise, $a_{ij}=0$.

$$\begin{bmatrix} 0 & 1 & 0 & 0 & 1 \\ 0 & 0 & 1 & 0 & 0 \\ 0 & 0 & 0 & 1 & 0 \\ 0 & 0 & 0 & 0 & 0 \\ 0 & 0 & 0 & 1 & 0 \end{bmatrix}$$

Figure 6.6 - *The adjacency matrix for the graph in Figure 6.1.*

For our purposes the powers[53] of adjacency matrix are especially interesting. The entry in column i and row j of the adjacency matrix raised in the n-th power is the number of paths of length n from node i to node j.

$$\begin{bmatrix} 0 & 0 & 1 & 1 & 0 \\ 0 & 0 & 0 & 1 & 0 \\ 0 & 0 & 0 & 0 & 0 \\ 0 & 0 & 0 & 0 & 0 \\ 0 & 0 & 0 & 0 & 0 \end{bmatrix}$$

Figure 6.7 - *The adjacency matrix for the graph in Figure 6.1 squared. The $a13 = 1$ indicates that there is one path of length 2 from node 1 to node 3.*

Although the square of the adjacency matrix in Figure 6.7 is the adjacency matrix of the graph shown in Figure 6.8, in general, the power of the adjacency matrix does not have be an adjacency matrix anymore.

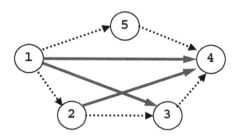

Figure 6.8 - *Graph corresponding to the adjacency matrix in Figure 6.1.*

There are various ways to fix this problem, and these ways will be explained   later. For now, given the adjacency matrix A, consider a formal series:

---

[53] Matrix power A^{n} is the product of n copies of A: $A^{n} = A \cdot A \cdot A \cdot \dots \cdot A$

$$T_A = A + A^2 + A^3 + \ldots$$

By adding the matrix powers A^n what kind of matrix T_A is produced? The reader can easily convince himself that an entry in column i, row j of matrix A^n is the number of paths of length n from node i to node j in the original graph. Then, an entry in matrix T_A is the number of paths of any length from node i to node j.

For adjacency matrices corresponding to directed acyclic graphs the powers would evaluate to 0 for a sufficiently large n, and the formal series T_A is finite. In other words, all the paths in a directed acyclic graph have their length bounded.

Given a transitive closure series matrix T_A, if any nonzero number is changed into 1, then T_A can be converted and obtained into an adjacency matrix!

$$T_A = \begin{bmatrix} 0 & 1 & 1 & 2 & 1 \\ 0 & 0 & 1 & 1 & 0 \\ 0 & 0 & 0 & 1 & 0 \\ 0 & 0 & 0 & 0 & 0 \\ 0 & 0 & 0 & 1 & 0 \end{bmatrix}$$

Figure 6.9 - *Example with graph at Figure 6.1 continued: Matrix T_A can be converted to the adjacency matrix for a transitive closure by changing the value 2 into 1. All other matrix entries remain unchanged.*

Next, the matrix powers sum is arranged a little bit differently:

$$T_A = A + A\,(A + A^2 + A^3 + \ldots)$$

The series in the parenthesis is again T_A, hence:

$$T_A = A + A\ T_A$$

It is this expression that is compared against the recursive *with* query in the beginning of the section. First, consider the product of matrices A and T_A. Matrix multiplication in SQL can be expressed as:

```
table A (
   i    integer, -- column i
   j    integer, -- column j
   val number    -- value of A(i,j)
);
table T_A (
   i    integer,
   j    integer,
   val number
);

select A.i AS i, T_A.j AS j, sum(A.val*T_A.val) AS val
from A, T
where A.j=T_A.i
group by A.i, T_A.j
```

The join between A and T_A looks similar to the join between *Edges* and *TransClosedEdges* in the recursive SQL query that was introduced in the beginning of the section. It is the aggregation part that appears to make them look alike.

This is not the only way to multiply the matrices in SQL, however. Remember that products and sums of adjacency matrices have nonnegative integer entries. Therefore, instead of having a single row *(i,j,val)*, we can have a bag of *val* identical rows of *(i,j)*. Schema design, once again, is important!

SQL operates with bags of values, which are not much different from numbers in base-1 number system. Any record with a nonnegative count field can be converted into a bag of identical records without this field. Bags are added with the *union all* operator, e.g.

```
select head, tail from Edges1
union all
select head, tail from Edges2
we multiply them with Cartesian product, e.g.
select e1.head, e1.tail, e2.head, e2.tail
from Edges1 e1, Edges2 e2
```

The bag result could be aggregated back into a set of records (by counting).

In a bag design matrix, multiplication reduces to:

```
table A (
    i    integer,  -- column i
    j    integer   -- column j
);
table T_A (
    i    integer,
    j    integer
);

select A.i AS i, T_A.j AS j
from A, T
where A.j=T_A.i
```

The right side of the equation that defines a transitive closure

$$T_A = A + A \, T_A$$

could be written in full in SQL as:

```
select i, j
from A
union all
select A.i AS i, T_A.j AS j
from A, T
where A.j=T_A.i
```

After renaming variables appropriately, it becomes indistinguishable from the recursive view *TransClosedEdges* definition in the query:

```
with TransClosedEdges (tail, head) as
( select tail, head from Edges
  union all
  select e.tail, ee.head from Edges e, TransClosedEdges ee
  where e.head = ee.tail
)
select distinct * from TransClosedEdges
```

The outer query transforms a bag back into a set because it is of interest to know if there are paths from *node* tail to node *head*, rather than their exact number.

Given the matrix interpretation of the recursive transitive closure query, the matrix evaluation can be translated into the SQL execution steps as follows:

Step	Matrix	SQL
1: Initialization	$T_A := A$	`TransClosedEdges :=` `select tail, head from Edges`

2: Temporary product	$P := A\,T_A$	`P :=`
		`select e.tail, ee.head from Edges`
		`e, TransClosedEdges ee`
		`where e.head = ee.tail`

3: Conditional termination	$P = 0$?
	
	return T_A
		`P = ∅ ?`
		
		`return TransClosedEdges`

4: Iteration	$T_A := A + P$	`TransClosedEdges :=`
		`select tail, head from Edges`
		`union all`
		`P`

A reader who is already familiar with the recursive SQL from another source may have already learned an entirely different algorithm. SQL, however, is about declarative programming and not about the algorithms. Any algorithm would do as long as it produces the correct result set. Recursive SQL is known to have many execution strategies:

---

naïve, incremental (semi-naïve), etc. Our algorithm could be coined as matrix evaluation.

There is a pitfall, however. The query would never terminate on graphs with cycles. Indeed, a cycle that passes through node i would eventually produce the edge *(tail=i, head=i)* in the *TransClosedEdges* relation. The *TransClosedEdges* relation never shrinks; therefore this record would remain in the *TransClosedEdges*. Then, the join at step 2 would never be empty.

One of the solutions to the cycle problem is suggested in the *DB2 Cookbook* by Graeme Birchall[54]. Recursive *with* construction is very powerful since extra columns may be introduced and those columns would be calculated recursively! One such column fits naturally into our query – the path expression:

```
with TransClosedEdges (tail, head) as
( select tail, head, tail||'.'||head AS path
  from Edges
  union all
  select e.tail, ee.head, e.tail||'.'||ee.path AS path
  from Edges e, TransClosedEdges ee
  where e.head = ee.tail
)
select distinct * from TransClosedEdges
```

Then Graeme goes on introducing a function called *LOCATE_BLOCK*, which could be used in the *where* clause as an indicator that the current node is in the path already:

```
with TransClosedEdges (tail, head) as
( select tail, head, tail||'.'||head AS path
  from Edges
  union all
  select e.tail, ee.head, e.tail||'.'||ee.path AS path
  from Edges e, TransClosedEdges ee
where e.head = ee.tail
```

---

[54] A similar solution has been implemented by Serge Rielau. If you are DB2 user, chances are that his CONNECT_BY_NOCYCLE function is a part of the database engine already. Otherwise, download it from IBM developerWorks website.

```
and LOCATE_BLOCK(e.head, path) = 0
)
select distinct * from TransClosedEdges
```

There is a more satisfactory solution to the cycle problem, though. Both DB2 and SQL Server slightly deviated from the ANSI SQL standard which demands a union in the recursive query definition. With the set semantics, the transitive closure relation *TransClosedEdges* cannot grow larger than a complete graph -- a graph in which every pair of nodes is connected.

Let's complete the section with simple wisdom about performance. Clearly, the *Edges.head* column has to be indexed if this query is to be scaled to a hierarchy of any significant size. The same comment applies to the Oracle solution discussed next.

Connect By

There are several ways to query a transitive closure in Oracle, beginning with parsing the *sys_connect_by_path* pseudo column and ending with firing the corellated *connect by* subquery:

```
select a.tail, b.head from Edges a, Edges b
where b.head in (
      select head from Edges
      connect by prior head = tail
      start with tail = a.tail
)
```

Without question the most satisfactory method both aesthetically and performance-wise is:

```
select connect_by_root(tail), tail
from Edges
connect by prior head = tail
```

This transitive closure query is succinct, but still the syntax could be improved. Apparently, the designers were preoccupied with tree problems, hence the *connect_by_root* pseudo column. There is no concept of the root node anywhere in the transitive closure problem scope.

Likewise, the concept of the *prior* edge belongs to the solution space rather than is inherent to the transitive closure problem. Overall, the transitive closure is defined symmetrically in terms of the *head* and *tail*, but the query above is skewed.

The cycle issue is no-brainer, as there is a dedicated keyword to take care of it:

```
select connect_by_root(tail), tail
from Edges
connect by nocycle prior head = tail
```

Incremental Evaluation

Transitive closure enjoys a lot of attention in the database research community. Proving the impossibility of doing things in a certain way is one of the favorite theoretical topics. Not surprisingly, it was established very early that transitive closure cannot be expressed by simple means of relational algebra, even enhanced with aggregation and grouping.

We have already seen the power of the incremental evaluation idea in the database implementation world. Indexes and materialized views are the most familiar incremental evaluation structures. *Dong et al*[55] proved that transitive closure can be efficiently maintained via an incremental evaluation system. In this section Dong's approach is explored, although with some deviation that would simplify the matter.

Let's revisit the transitive closure expression in terms of the adjacency matrix:

$$T = A + A^2 + A^3 + ...$$

From a mathematical perspective this is quite a handsome series. It could be made even prettier if we consider the *identity matrix* – the matrix

---

[55] G. Dong, L. Libkin, J. Su and L. Wong. Maintaining the transitive closure of graphs in SQL. http://citeseer.ist.psu.edu/dong99maintaining.html

with ones on the main diagonal and zeros elsewhere. A common notation for the identity matrix is symbol 1. Perhaps the most important equality involving the identity matrix is:

$$1 = A^0$$

There it shows that the identity matrix literally begs to be added in front of the series for the transitive closure:

$$T = 1 + A + A^2 + A^3 + ...$$

Speaking in graph language, what happened is the loops were included at each node. Formally, T is now both a reflexive and transitive closure.

Are there any immediate benefits? Let's multiply[56] T by $1 - A$

$$T(1 - A) = 1 + A + A^2 + A^3 + ... - (A + A^2 + A^3 + ...)$$

All the nonzero powers of A at the right side cancel out:

$$T(1 - A) = 1$$

Multiplying both sides by the inverse of $1 - A$ gives an explicit formula for the transitive closure:

$$T = (1 - A)^{-1}$$

Therefore, we might be able to calculate transitive closure (of directed acyclic graphs, at least), if we know how to invert matrices in SQL! Unfortunately, inverting matrices in SQL is difficult. The matrix

---

[56] Usually, when speaking matrix multiplication we have to be careful, since matrix product is not commutative, and clarify if we meant the left or right multiplication. In this case it doesn't matter, so we can afford a sloppy language.

approach, however, still shows its practical merit in the scope of an incremental evaluation system.

In the incremental evaluation method, the original graph is stored together with another graph -- its transitive closure. Every time the original graph is updated that is a new edge is inserted or deleted; the transitive closure graph has to be changed as well so that the information in both structures remains consistent. The problem of *transitive closure graph maintenance* essentially is finding an efficient SQL expression for the insertions and deletions in the transitive closure graph.

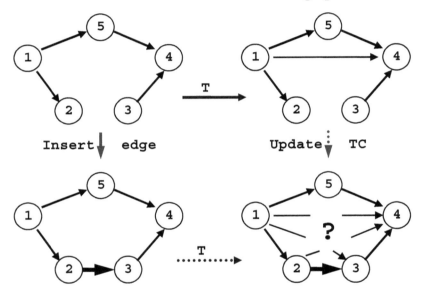

Figure 6.10 - *Transitive closure graph maintenance problem: Inserting the edge (2,3) into the graph at the top left, is expected to update the transitive closure structure at the top right accordingly.*

Let's continue pursuing the adjacency matrix approach. Inserting an edge *(x,y)* into the original graph produces a new graph with the adjacency matrix

$$A + S$$

that is the original matrix A incremented by S, the latter being a matrix with a single nonzero entry in column x, row y. How would this increment of the adjacency matrix affect the transitive closure matrix? Well, let's calculate. The new transitive closure matrix is:

$$1 + A + S + (A + S)^2 + (A + S)^3 + \dots$$

Expanding powers into polynomials[57] the result is:

$$1 + (A + S) + (A^2 + AS + SA + S^2) +$$
$$+ (A^3 + A^2 S + ASA + AS^2 + SA^2 + SAS + S^2 A + S^3) + \dots$$

Let's rearrange terms more suggestively:

$$1 + A + A^2 + A^3 + \dots + (S + AS + SA + A^2 S + ASA + SA^2 + \dots) +$$
$$+ (S^2 + AS^2 + SAS + S^2 A + S^3 + \dots)$$

The first series is the familiar transitive closure matrix T of the original not incremented adjacency matrix A. The second series could be factored into

$$(1 + A + A^2 + A^3 + \dots) S (1 + A + A^2 + A^3 + \dots)$$

which reduces to T S T. The last series vanishes if the scope is limited to directed acyclic graphs. Indeed, each term in that series is multiplied by S at least twice. In other words, each term in the series corresponds to a path in the graph that goes through the edge *(x,y)* twice, which implies a cycle.

Summarizing, the new transitive closure matrix reduces to:

$$T + TST$$

Incremental Maintenance of Graph Matrices

---

[57] Careful with matrix multiplication being non-commutative!

> When the original adjacency matrix A is incremented by S, the transitive closure matrix T is incremented by T S T.

This is a very succinct result. The result is double checked by comparing it with the query computing the transitive closure increment in Dong's paper:

```
SELECT *
FROM (
        SELECT VALUES (a, b)
    UNION
        SELECT Start = TC.Start, End = b
        FROM TC
        WHERE TC.End = a
    UNION
        SELECT Start = a, End = TC.End
        FROM TC
        WHERE b = TC.Start
    UNION
        SELECT Start = TC1.Start, End = TC2.End
        FROM TC AS TC1, TC AS TC2
        WHERE TC1.End = a AND TC2.Start = b
) AS T;

SELECT *
FROM TC-NEW AS T
WHERE NOT EXISTS (SELECT *
                  FROM TC
                  WHERE TC.Start=T.Start AND TC.End=T.End)
INTO TEMP DELTA;

INSERT INTO TC
SELECT *
FROM DELTA;
```

The first part of the query, which is a union of four blocks is supposed to correspond to the transitive closure matrix increment T S T. It appears that they are very dissimilar. How can this be?

Remember, however, that we conveniently decided to operate the reflexive transitive closure matrices. If we go back and represent T as $1+T'$, where T' is not reflexive anymore, then the increment matrix has to be written as $(1+T') S (1+T')$ which can be expanded into

$$S + T'S + S T' + T'S T'$$

with four terms as in Dong's method.

Now that we are confident with the matrix solution, it can be finalized in terms of SQL. It has already been shown the operating matrices of integers that count paths in the directed acyclic graph offers an exceptional clarity. Therefore, let's represent the transitive closure relation directly after the transitive closure matrix that was investigated earlier:

```
table TRC (       -- transitive, reflexive closure
   i    integer, -- tail
   j    integer, -- head
   val integer   -- weight
)
```

Once again, it is the reflexive property and the additional information in the *val* column that distinguishes this method formally from Dong's.

However, there is an ambiguity. What about zero matrix entries? There is an option available to either store it as *(i,j,0)* or ignore such rows. The first option simplifies SQL that maintains the table *TRC*. The second option provides a natural means for compressing sparse matrices.

Sparse Matrices

Sparse matrices save space. Instead of storing full matrix

```
i j val
-- ---
1 1  0
1 2  0
1 3  1
2 1  0
2 2  0
2 3  0
3 1  0
3 2  5
3 3  0
```

it is more economical to omit zero entries

```
i j val
```

```
-- ---
13  1
32  5
```

Now all the ground work for transitive closure maintenance in SQL is complete. Inserting an edge *(x,y)* into the adjacency graph has to trigger a conforming change in the transitive closure table *TRC*. The values in the *TRC.val* column should be incremented accordingly by the entries of the product of three matrices T S T.

Knowing how to write a product of two arbitrary matrices in SQL, the product of three matrices -- A B C -- can be written as a composition of two binary product operations (A B) C. Alternatively, matrix elements are summed up at once

$$\sum_l \left(\sum_k a_{ik} \, b_{kl} \right) c_{lj} = \sum_{k,l} a_{ik} \, b_{kl} \, c_{lj}$$

which is easy to translate into SQL:

```
select A.i AS i, C.j AS j, sum(A.val*B.val*C.val) AS val
from A, B, C
where A.j=B.i and B.j=C.i
group by A.i, C.j
```

Please note how naturally the matrix associativity property goes along with the relational join associativity.

Actually, the goal is a simpler matrix product -- T S T. There is no challenge adapting the general case to our needs:

```
select t1.i AS i, t2.j AS j, sum(t1.val*t2.val) AS val
from TRC t1, TRC t2
where t1.j = :x and t2.i = :y
group by t1.i, t2.j
```

If the option of storing zero matrix entries is chosen, then the above query fits naturally into an update statement to the *TRC* table:

```
update TRC
set val = (
   select val + sum(t1.val*t2.val)
   from TRC t1, TRC t2
   where t1.j = :x and t2.i = :y
   and t1.i = trc.i, t2.j = trc.j
   group by t1.i, t2.j
)
```

It is fascinating that the transitive closure table maintenance is solvable with a single update, but this answer is unrealistic for two reasons. First, the *TRC* table has to grow at some moment, and this issue is left out of scope. Second, from a performance perspective, updating or trying to update all the rows in the *TRC* table smells a disaster. It would be helpful to know which rows require update, and formalize it within the *where* clause (which is entirely missing).

Therefore, let's materialize updates to the TRC table in a designated table *TRCDelta*:

```
insert into TRCDelta
select t1.i AS i, t2.j AS j, sum(t1.val*t2.val) AS val
from TRC t1, TRC t2
where t1.j = :x and t2.i = :y
group by t1.i, t2.j
```

To keep this table small, matrix entries should not be stored with zero values any longer. On the other hand, by just storing a sparse matrix stored in the *TRC* table, the *TRCDelta* is automatically calculated as a sparse matrix either.

It is the *TRC* table update step that has to be adjusted. There are two cases:

- All the rows in *TRCDelta* that do not match *TRC* rows have to be inserted:

  ```
  insert into TRC
  ```

```
select * from TRCDelta
where (i,j) not in (select i,j from TRC)
```

- The rows that match have to increment their values:

```
update TRC
set val = val + (select val from TRCDelta td
                    where td.i = trc.i and td.j = trc.j)
where (i,j) in (select i,j from TRCDelta)
```

This completes the program in the case of an insertion of an edge. What about a deletion? From the matrix perspective the cases of inserting an edge and deleting it are symmetric. Following the earlier development, the same matrix S that corresponds to a single edge *(x,y)* *could be used*, except that it must be subtracted everywhere. The final result in the matrix form is that transitive closure matrix T is decremented by T S T.

In the first naïve update solution for the *TRC* table all that must be done is to reverse the sign:

```
update TRC
set val = (
    select val - sum(t1.val*t2.val)
    from TRC t1, TRC t2
    where t1.j = :x and t2.i = :y
    and t1.i = trc.i, t2.j = trc.j
    group by t1.i, t2.j
)
```

Please note, that this symmetry is made possible because of the extra information that was stored in the *TRC* table. Since the number of paths that are going from node *i* to node *j is known*, all the paths that are affected by the deletion of an edge *(x,y) can simply be subtracted*. In Dong's approach, maintenance under deletion is more complicated.

Carrying over the solution to sparse matrices requires little insight. The *TRCDelta* table that stores the T S T matrix is calculated the same way as in the edge insertion scenario. Thus, subtracting the T S T from T brings up two possibilities:

- An entry in the transitive closure matrix T is the same as the corresponding entry in the T S T.

- An entry in the transitive closure matrix T is bigger than the corresponding entry in the T S T.

In the first case the entry in the difference matrix T − T S T is *0*. Therefore, all these entries have to be deleted:

```
delete from TRC
where (i,j, val) in (select i,j, val from TRCDelta)
```

All the other entries have to be adjusted:

```
update TRC
set val = val - (select val from TRCDelta td
                where td.i = trc.i and td.j = trc.j)
where (i,j) in (select i,j from TRCDelta)
```

Now that several methods for transitive closure calculation/ maintenance has been shown, let's again return to applications. Perhaps the most significant problem that can be expressed in terms of transitive closure is aggregation on graphs.

Hierarchical Weighted Total

Before exploring aggregation on graphs, let's have a quick look at aggregation on trees. Aggregation on trees is much simpler and has a designated name: hierarchical total. A typical query is:

Find combined salary of all the employees under direct and indirect supervision of King.

This query, however, has no inherent complexity, and it effectively reduces to the familiar task of finding a set of all the node's descendants.

In graph context, the hierarchical total query is commonly referred to as the bill of materials (BOM). Consider bicycle parts assembly:

Part	SubPart	Quantity
Bicycle	Wheel	2
Wheel	Reflector	2
Bicycle	Frame	1
Frame	Reflector[58]	2

Parts with the same name are assumed to be identical. They are modeled as nodes in an acyclic directed graph. The edges specify the construction flow:

- Assemble each wheel from the required parts (including reflectors).

- Assemble the frame from the required components (including reflectors).

- Assemble a bicycle from the required parts (including frame and wheels).

Suppose the total list of parts for the bike assembly is to be ordered. How is the quantity for each part calculated? Unlike the hierarchical total for a tree, the quantities cannot simply be added as they multiply along each path.

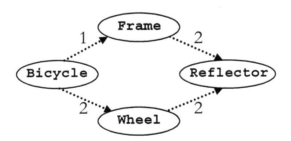

Figure 6.11 - *Bicycle assembly graph. The total number of reflector parts should be calculated as the sum of parts aggregated along each path. The path*

---

[58] Actually, both frame reflectors have different colors (red and silver). Also, they are different in shape and color from the reflectors that are mounted on wheels. To make example more interesting we assume all of them to be identical.

/Bicycle/Wheel/Reflector contributes to 2*2=4 parts: bicycle has 2 wheels, each wheel has 2 reflectors. Likewise, the path /Bicycle/Frame/Reflector contribute to 1*2=2 more parts.

Therefore, there are two levels of aggregation here, multiplication of the quantities along each path and summation along each alternative path.

Aggregation on Graphs

Two levels of aggregation fit naturally into in graphs queries. Consider finding a shortest path between two nodes. First, the distances are added along each path, and a path is chosen with minimal length.

Double aggregation is not something unique to graph queries, however. Consider the following query:

Find the sum of the salaries grouped by department. Select maximum of them.

When expressing such a query in SQL, the first sentence is accommodated as an inner subquery inside the outer query corresponding to the second sentence:

```
select max(salaryExpences) from (
    select deptno, sum(sal) salaryExpenses
    from Emp
    group by dept
)
```

The hierarchical weighted total query has the same structure. The first level of aggregation where edges are joined into paths is analogous to the *group by* subquery from the salary expense query. Formally, it is a transitive closure, which is enhanced with additional aggregates or a generalized transitive closure.

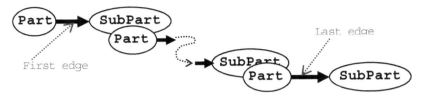

Figure 6.12 - *Generalized transitive closure. There are several aggregates naturally associated with each path: the first edge, the last edge, the path length, or any aggregate on the edge weights.*

The following is a hypothetical SQL syntax for a generalized transitive closure:

```
select distinct first(Part), last(SubPart), product (Quantity)
from AssemblyEdges
connect by prior Part = later SubPart
```

The unfamiliar syntax requires some clarification:

- The *product* is a non-standard aggregate from Chapter 4.

- The *first* and *last* refer to the first and last edges in the path, correspondingly. These aggregates are unique to ordered structures such as directed graphs.

- Although not used in the example, concatenating edge labels into a string is one more natural aggregation function, which is unique to graphs. The *list* aggregate function is a standard way to accommodate it.

- The *later* keyword is just a syntactic sugar fixing apparent asymmetry caused by the *prior* keyword.

- There is no *start with* clause, which is, in fact, redundant. It is an outer query where paths will be restricted to those originated in the *'Bicycle'* node.

The generalized transitive closure query is enveloped with a second level of aggregation, which is accomplished by standard means:

```
select leaf, sum(factoredQuantity) from (
   select product(Quantity) factoredQuantity,
          first(Part) root, last(SubPart) leaf
   from AssemblyEdges
   connect by prior Part = later SubPart
) where root = 'Bicycle'
group by leaf
```

Enough theory, so what is done in the real world to implement an aggregated weighted total query? Let's start with Oracle, because the proposed syntax for a generalized transitive closure resembles the Oracle *connect by*.

First, we have to be able to refer to the first and the last edges in the path:

```
select connect_by_root(Part) root, SubPart leaf
from AssemblyEdges
connect by prior Part = SubPart
```

Unlike the fictional syntax, Oracle treats edges in the path asymmetrically. Any column from the *AssemblyEdges* table is assumed to implicitly refer to the last edge. This design dates back to version 7. The *connect_by_root* function referring to the first edge has been added in version 10. It is remarkable how this essentially ad-hock design proved to be successful in practice.

Next, Oracle syntax has several more path aggregate functions:

- *level* – the length of the path.

- *sys_connect_by_path* – essentially the *list* aggregate in the fictitious syntax.

- *connect_by_is_leaf* – an indicator if there is no paths which contain the current path as a prefix.

- *connect_by_is_cycle* – an indicator if the first edge is adjacent to the last.

Unfortunately, we need an aggregate which is a product[59] of edge weights and not a string which is a concatenation of weights produced by *sys_connect_by_path*. You might be tempted to hack a function which accepts a string of the edge weights, parses it, and returns the required aggregate value.

Nah, too easy! Can the problem be solved without coding a function even a simple one? Yes it can, although this solution would hardly be more efficient. The critical idea is representing any path in the graph as a concatenation of three paths:

- a prefix path from the start node to some intermediate node *i*

- a path consisting of a single weighted edge *(i,j)*

- a postfix path from the node *i* to the end node

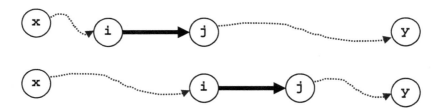

Figure 6.13 - *A path from node x to node y is a composition of the path from node x to node i, the edge (i, j), and the path from j to y. The edge (i, j) can be positioned anywhere along the path from x to y.*

Then, the path from *x* to *y is frozen* while interpreting the edge *(i,j)* as a variable. All that needs done is to aggregate the weights of all those edges.

---

[59] Or sum. In general, any multiplicative problem can be converted into addition by applying logarithm function.

Let's assemble the solution piece by piece. First, all the paths in the graphs are expressed as:

```
with TClosure as (
    select distinct connect_by_root(Part) x, SubPart y,
        sys_connect_by_path('['||Part||','||SubPart||'>',' ') path
    from AssemblyEdges
    connect by nocycle Part=prior SubPart
    union
    select Part, Part, '' from AssemblyEdges
    union
    select SubPart, SubPart, '' from AssemblyEdges
) …
```

This is essentially a reflexive transitive closure relation enhanced with the path column. Paths are strings of concatenated edges; each edge is sugarcoated into '['||Part||','||SubPart||'>', which helps visual perception, but is inessential for the solution.

Next, the two paths and the intermediate edge are joined together and grouped by paths:

```
… , PathQuantities as (
    select t1.x, t2.y,
        t1.p||' ['||e.Part||','||e.SubPart||'>'||t2.p,
        product(Quantity) Quantity
    from TClosure t1, AssemblyEdges e, TClosure t2
    where t1.y = e.Part and e.SubPart = t2.x
    group by t1.x, t2.y, t1.p||' ['||e.Part||','||e.SubPart||'>'||t2.p) …
```

Now all the paths with quantities aggregated along them are available. Let's group the paths by the first and last node in the path while adding the quantities:

```
select x, y, sum(Quantity)
from PathQuantities
group by x, y
```

This query is almost final, it needs only a minor touch: restricting the node *x* to *'Bicycle'* and interpreting the *y* column as a *Part* in the assembly:

```
select y Part, sum(Quantity)
from PathQuantities
where x = 'Bicycle'
group by x, y
```

The recursive SQL solution turns out to be quite satisfactory:

```
with TCAssembly as (
    select Part, SubPart, Quantity AS factoredQuantity
    from AssemblyEdges
    where Part = 'Bicycle'
    union all
    select te.Part, e.SubPart, e.Quantity * te.factoredQuantity
    from TCAssembly te, AssemblyEdges e
    where te.SubPart = e.Part
) select SubPart, sum(Quantity) from TCAssembly group by SubPart
```

Most importantly, it accommodates the inner aggregation with the non-standard aggregate effortlessly! The cycle detection issue that plagued the recursive SQL in the section on transitive closure is not a problem for the directed acyclic graphs.

The hierarchical total turns out to be surprisingly useful in the following two sections. Selecting all the subsets of items satisfying some aggregate criteria, *Basket* generation, appears to have little to do with the hierarchical total, at first. The other, rather unexpected application is *Comparing* hierarchies.

Generating Baskets

Given a set of items, how much, say, would $500 buy?

```
select * from items;
```

NAME	PRICE
monitor	400
printer	200
notebook	800
camera	300
router	30
microwave	80

Even though the problem may sound unbelievably simple, the answer involves finding all sets of items, not just the item records that cost below $500. However, what do those sets have to do with the graph problems that are the focus of this chapter? Well, there is no method on how to generate sets of items, but even if there were, the second challenge would be aggregating a price on these sets[60].

The problem in terms of graphs is reformulated using the very suggestive Figure 6.14 as the basic idea.

Figure 6.14 - *Price aggregation on the set {camera, monitor, notebook} can be viewed as a hierarchical total on a graph.*

What criterion connects the items in the graph? Anything that does not list an item twice would do. For purposes in this chapter, any two items are connected if the first item precedes lexicographically to the second one. Then, as in the hierarchical total section, the solution has to branch in order to accommodate the differences between various platforms.

In Oracle the idea is adopted from Figure 6.13. Unlike the previous section, however, where values were aggregated on edges, values are added together on nodes. The path is decomposed into the three components as shown in Figure 6.15.

---

[60] A familiar *group by* clause does aggregate on sets, but those sets are required to be **disjoint**.

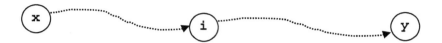

Figure 6.15 - *A path from node x to node y is a composition of the path from node x to node i, the node i, and the path from i to y. Summation of the weights assigned to all such nodes i produces the aggregate weight of the path .*

The transitive closure relation together with an aggregation query formally is:

```
with Sets as (
   select distinct connect_by_root(name) x, name y,
      case when connect_by_root(name) = name then
         ' '
      else
         substr(sys_connect_by_path(name,','),
           instr(sys_connect_by_path(name,','),',',2))
      end p
   from items
   connect by nocycle name > prior name
), SetTotals as (
   select t1.x||t1.p||t2.p,
   sum(price) price_sum
   from Sets t1, Items i, Sets t2
   where t1.y = i.name and i.name = t2.x
   group by t1.x||t1.p||t2.p
)
```

Most of the attention here has been focused on making the path string look right. Without this twisted *case* condition, joining the paths according to Figure 6.15 would produce strings with duplicate items, e.g. *camera, camera, monitor.*

The final query is now one step away:

```
select * from SetTotals
where price_sum < 500
```

T1.X||T1.P||T2.P	PRICE SUM
microwave	80
microwave,printer,router	310
microwave,monitor	480
camera	300
microwave,printer	280
printer	200
camera,microwave,router	410
monitor,router	430
printer,router	230
microwave,router	110
camera,microwave	380
camera,router	330
monitor	400
router	30

Now that the *connect by* based solution has been examined, let's see what recursive SQL can offer. The solution is embarrassingly simple:

```
with Sets (maxName, itemSet, sumPrice) as (
select name, name, price
union
select name, itemSet || ',' name, sumPrice + price
from Sets, T
where name > maxName
and sumPrice + price < 500
) select itemSet, sumPrice from Sets
```

Not only it is clearer, but it is also more efficient. Imagine a store with 50K items. Calculating all the subsets of the items is not a proposition that is expected to be completed in the remaining lifetime of the universe. The number of baskets with the aggregated cost limited by some modest amount, however, is reasonably small. Once again, applying predicates early is a good idea in general.

Comparing Hierarchies

Being able to navigate graph structures is only a part of the story. Comparing hierarchies is more challenging. First of all, by what criteria are two hierarchical structures considered as equivalent? In particular, is the order of siblings important?

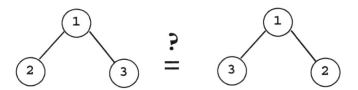

Figure 6.15 - *The first dilemma of tree comparison. Is reorganizing a tree by reordering siblings allowed?*

Depending on the context, the reader may lean to one or the other answer.

Likewise, can children become grandchildren?

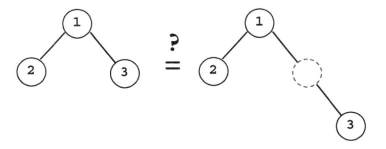

Figure 6.16 - *The second dilemma of tree comparison. Can a tree be restructured with an intermediate node in the chain of ancestors introduced?*

Even though a reader may lean to the conclusion that dummy intermediate nodes are not allowed, it is easy to provide a counter example when ignoring certain types of intermediate nodes is imperative.

This ambiguity is discouraging. Yet, let's ignore it for a while and try to develop some basic understanding of how trees can be compared. Looking desperately for a bright idea, I pulled the following entry from *thesaurus.com*

Main Entry: compare

Synonyms: analyze, approach, balance, bracket, collate, confront, consider, contemplate, correlate, divide, equal, examine, hang, inspect, juxtapose, match, match up, measure, observe, oppose, parallel, ponder, rival, scan, scrutinize, segregate, separate, set against, size up, study, touch, **weigh**

The last synonym – weigh – sounds promising. When comparing two things in the physical world, they are measured on some scale or weighed. Perhaps tree weights can be compared somehow?

Figure 6.17 - *Weighting trees.*

Let's revisit the idea of the hierarchical total. When calculating the total, a raw node weight is augmented by the augmented weights of its children. The process begins at the root node descending recursively down to the leaves. The trick is to guess the right kind of aggregation, which accommodates both the tree structure and unaugmented node weights. Then, for all comparison purposes a tree can be identified with the augmented weight of its root node.

The easiest aggregation to try is simply the sum of all tree node weights. This naïve method, however, fails to take into account the differences in the tree structure.

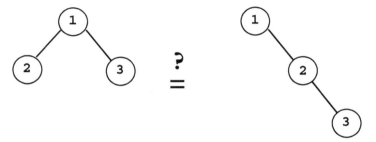

Figure 6.18 - *Adding node weights fails to distinguish tree structure. Both the tree on the left and the tree on the right have the same weight 1+2+3 = 6*

Joe Celko noticed that even though the weights at the root nodes are the same, the weights at node *2* are different. Thus a comparison is needed of the two sets of nodes element-by-element with their respective weights. This is easy enough to do; simply store the weights in *Table1*

AggregatedWeight
3
5
6

and *Table2*

AggregatedWeight
3
2
6

Then, check if the symmetric difference is empty.

```
select AggregatedWeight from Table1
minus
select AggregatedWeight from Table2
union
select AggregatedWeight from Table2
minus
select AggregatedWeight from Table1
```

Still, the idea of comparing scalar values rather than sets of values is very appealing. Sets of integers are well known to be mapped bijectively to ordinary integers. This may not be a practical solution, but at least it supports the intuition that a scalar based tree comparison is possible.

Why is the method of mapping integer sets into integers unpractical? First, tree nodes can be labeled with values of datypes other than integers. This is easily fixable, since the only important property of the label for tree comparison purposes is its identity. Any value of any datatype can be mapped to an integer, and in fact such a map is commonly known as a *hash* function. Second, a much more difficult problem is that the mapping of sets integers to integers grows very fast. The range of computer integer numbers overflows pretty easily even for sets of a moderate size. A hash function, however, provides a satisfactory solution to the range overflowing problem as well.

The basic premise of any hash-based method is that the (unlikely) hash code collisions are tolerable. Given an object a, the chance that there exists another object $x \neq a$ such that $hash(a)=hash(x)$ is considered as negligible. Likewise, for any objects a, b, x and y satisfying the equation $hash(a)+hash(b)=hash(x)+hash(y)$ it must either follow that $x=a$, $y=b$ or $x=b$, $y=a$. This could be contrasted to the ordinary addition wherein the equation $a+b=x+y$ is too ambiguous to determine x and y.

The hierarchical total query can be defined recursively. At each node labeled p, which has children $c1$, $c2$, ..., cn, we aggregate the following value:

$$total(p) = hash(p+total(c_1)+total(c_2)+\ldots+total(c_n))$$

The recursive definition is the easiest to implement with recursive SQL. Consider the employee hierarchy:

```
table Employees ( -- tree nodes
    id   integer primary key,
    sal  integer
);

table Subordination ( -- tree edges
   mgr integer references Employees,
   emp integer references Employees
);
```

Then, the hierarchical total query starts with the leaf nodes:

```
select id, hash(id) AS total
from Employees
where id not in (select mgr from Subordination)
```

The recursive step mimics the recurrence definition:

```
with NodeWeights as (
   select id, hash(id) AS total
   from Employees
   where id not in (select mgr from Subordination)
    union all
   select e.id, e.id+sum(hash(total))
   from Subordination s, Employees e, NodeWeights nw
   where s.mgr = e.id and s.emp = nw.id
   group by e.id
) select weight from NodeWeights
where id not in (select emp from Subordination)
```

After all hierarchy nodes are weighted, the outermost query selects the weight at the root node.

It is difficult to fit a recursive idea into the *connect by* framework. Likewise, when nested sets and intervals were studied, the recursive ideas were ignored altogether. Could the hash based tree comparison method be adapted to these contexts as well?

Let's invoke our familiar path encoding – after all, it reflects a tree structure. Admittedly, I do not know how to aggregate paths in a subtree of descendants, but I can suggest adding their hash values instead! More specifically, a hash value of each node can be multiplied by a hash value of the node path and summed up the hierarchy. This definition is free of recursion, and therefore, is exactly what is required for the hierarchical total method to work.

The method for basic tree comparison can be amended to meet the exact tree equality specification. In the beginning of the section there were two tree equality dilemmas that were left hanging. In the first dilemma, if the reordering of siblings is allowed, the node summation is performed exactly as described. Otherwise, the node weights should be multiplied by the order numbers.

For example, for the left tree in Figure 6.14 the augmented weight of the root node has to be recalculated to become *1*1 + 2*1 + 3*2 = 7*. If leaves *2* and *3* are swapped, then the weight at the root node has to change to *1*1 + 3*1 + 2*2 = 8*. A similar idea applies to the hash-based comparison method, where the hierarchical total formula becomes:

$$total(p) = hash(p + 1 \cdot total(c_1) + 2 \cdot total(c_2) + \ldots + n \cdot total(c_n))$$

Likewise, in the second dilemma if intermediate empty nodes in the tree structure are allowed, then Celko's method works as it is. Otherwise, each unaugmented node weight is multiplied by the level. For example, for the left tree in Figure 6.15 the augmented weight of the root node has to be recalculated to become *1*1 + 2*2 + 2*3 = 11*. For the right tree it is *1*1 + 2*2 + 2*0 + 3*3 = 14*. By contrast, the hash-based tree comparison method considers the tree structures in Figure 6.15 as different.

Summary

- Learning transitive closure is essential for mastering queries on graphs.

- If you are implementing incrementally maintained transitive closure, then consider using the matrix method.

- The hierarchical weighted total query has two levels of aggregation.

- Hierarchical total can be leveraged for tree comparison.

Adjacency relation (tree edges; standalone, or combined with the tree nodes)	Nested Sets	Materialized Path	Nested Intervals via Matrix encoding
Have to use **proprietory** SQL extensions for finding ancestors and descendants; although the queries are efficient	Standard SQL	Standard SQL	Standard SQL
Finding descendants is relatively efficient (i.e. proportional to the size of the subtree)	Finding descendants is easy and relatively efficient (i.e. proportional to the size of the subtree)	Finding descendants is easy and relatively efficient (i.e. proportional to the size of the subtree)	Same as MP: Finding descendants is easy and relatively efficient
Finding ancestors is efficient	Finding ancestors is easy but inefficient	Finding ancestors is tricky but efficient	Same as MP: Finding ancestors is tricky but efficient
Finding node's children is trivial	Finding node's children as all the descendants restricted to the next level is inefficient	Finding node's children as descendants on next level is inefficient	Same as AR: Finding node's children is trivial

	(e.g. consider root node)		
Finding node's parent is trivial	Finding node's parent as ancestor on the previous level Is inefficient due to inefficiency of ancestors search	Finding node's parent as ancestor on the previous level is efficient	Same as AR: Finding node's parent is trivial
Aggregate queries are relatively efficient (i.e. proportional to the size of the subtree)	Aggregate queries are relatively efficient (except counting, which is super fast)!	Aggregate queries are relatively efficient (i.e. proportional to the size of the subtree)	Aggregate queries are relatively efficient (i.e. proportional to the size of the subtree)
Tree reorganization is very simple	Tree reorganization is hard	Tree reorganization is easy	Tree reorganization is easy (but not as simple as in AR)

Figure 6.18 - *Feature matrix of different hierarchy methods.*

Exercises

Exercise 1:

For many practical problems the *forest* data structure is more natural than tree. A forest is a set of disjoint trees, and it is a simpler concept than tree because it requires only two constraints. Which ones?

Exercise 2:

In graph theory tree is defined as a connected acyclic graph. Both concepts – tree and graph – are different from what was used in this chapter. In graph theory graphs are undirected and trees are not rooted. Does the graph theory perspective make defining tree constraints easier?

Exercise 3:

Adapt Graeme's cycle detection function *LOCATE_BLOCK* implementation to handle transitive closure for a graph with cycles.

Exercise 4:

Write a matrix summation query $A+B$ for sparse matrices A and B.

Exercise 5:

Some RDBMS offer a syntactic shortcut for combining an *insert* and *update* into a single SQL command – *merge*. Combine the *TRC* table maintenance operations together. Does the solution feel natural?

Exercise 6:

In the transitive closure maintenance under deletion, the *TRC* table could have been updated first and all zero entries wiped out. Write SQL commands implementing this idea.

Exercise 7:

Implement a function that accepts a string of numbers separated with a comma and returns the product of them. Write the hierarchical weighted total query that leverages it.

Exercise 8:

Write a query that finds the longest path between two nodes in a graph.

Exercise 9:

(Binomial coefficients continued). Any $x+y$ *choose* y entry in the Pascal triangle is a number of paths from the node $x=1, y=1$ to the node x, y (see the lattice picture below). Write a hierarchical total query that calculates a binomial coefficient.

Hint: build a lattice graph from the two sets of integers.

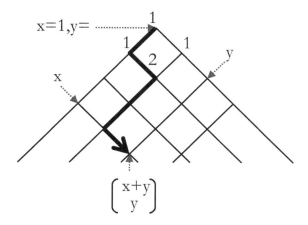

Exercise 10:

Applying predicates early is usually a good idea. In many cases no matter how the query is written, the optimizer would be able to push the predicate. A query block with the *connect by* clause is an exception. Reengineer the *connect by* solution for the hierarchical total query so that the root node is restricted to *'Bicycle'* as early as possible.

Exercise 11:

Implement the hash based path encoded tree comparison idea.

Exercise 12:

A labeled tree is determined by an unlabeled tree "the shape"

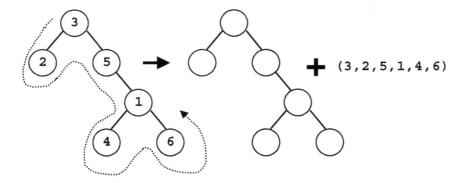

and by the sequence of node labels where nodes are traversed in some fixed order (say, preorder). An unlabeled tree is just a system of nested parenthesis, e.g. *(()((()()))*. Develop this fuzzy idea into a complete tree comparison method.

Exercise 13:

The topological sort of a DAG is a linear ordering of its nodes where each *head* node comes before all *tail* nodes. This definition is nondeterministic: for the graph in Figure 6.1 both *1,2,3,5,4* and *1,2,5,3,4* are valid topological sorts. It is impossible to express nondeterministic queries in SQL. Yet, it is easy to make the problem deterministic, requiring to find lexicographically smallest sequence among all possible topological sorts. Write a topological sort in SQL.   Hint: It is quite challenging to follow the above definition of a topological sort, since it involves a set of all legitimate topological sorts. Instead, approach the problem recursively. Find all the *head* nodes that are not listed as *tail* nodes. Enumerate them in increasing order. Reduce the problem to a smaller problem of finding the topological sort of the graph with all the edges that exclude the *head* nodes, which were considered at the last recursion step.

About Vadim Tropashko

Vadim Tropashko graduated from Moscow Institute of Physics and Technology in 1984. Tropashko researched Petri Nets for five years following graduation. In the early 90s, his interests switched to OOP. Tropashko translated "The C++ Programming Language" by B.Stroustrup into Russian. He was a C++ instructor at University of Radio and Electronics in Belarus. In the mid 90s, Tropashko's interest changed from OOP to databases. Vadim Tropashko has now worked for Oracle since 1998.

Index

www.ingramcontent.com/pod-product-compliance
Lightning Source LLC
Chambersburg PA
CBHW080401060326
40689CB00019B/4092